Angel
ORIGAMI

Angel ORIGAMI

15 Easy-to-Make Fun Paper Angels for Gifts or Keepsakes

NICK ROBINSON
Foreword by Chrissie Astell

WATKINS PUBLISHING
LONDON

Angel Origami
Nick Robinson

First published in the UK and USA in 2013 by
Watkins Publishing Limited
Sixth Floor
75 Wells Street
London W1T 3QH

A member of Osprey Group

Osprey Publishing Inc.
43-01 21st Street
Suite 220B, Long Island City
New York 11101

Managing Editor: Tania Ahsan
Managing Designer: Luana Gobbo
Commissioned Photography: Jules Selmes

A CIP record for this book is available from the British Library

ISBN: 978-1-78028-577-1
10 9 8 7 6 5 4 3 2 1

Typeset in Agenda and Chaparral Pro
Colour reproduction by PDQ, UK
Printed in China

Contents

"Fill your paper with the breathings of your heart."

WILLIAM WORDSWORTH (1770–1850)

Foreword

Some people are convinced that angels have been around since the beginning of time. They believe angels are part of the original creation and that, carrying the thoughts of God, they inspire in us awe at the beauty of the cosmos. This is in order that we, in turn, may learn to co-create with them, thus nurturing and caring for ourselves – and our planet.

More than ever, angels are appearing to us in amazing ways that capture our imagination and lift our spirits. We don't need to search far to discover angels in classical and modern art, in the lyrics of songs and in traditional religious hymns, sculptured in stone, carved into beautiful crystals, and depicted in films. From cave dwellers to great master painters, the "angelic muse" has inspired humanity for eons. Now, in our current era, we have available to us even more innovative and creative ways of gathering and producing images of angels. Angel origami is one such way of creating beautiful paper angels, made with love to represent the essence of angelic messages in a completely different way – and bring this blessing to your desk, your home or wherever else you would like to spread a little angelic energy.

We have grown accustomed to the recognizable form of graceful figures with wonderful swan-like white feather wings. This image, and its many variants, is perennially inspiring, even though the true essence of angels is more often experienced by people as different forms of energy, such as flickering waves or columns of light, a soft touching sensation on the skin, an audible sense of whispered messages or pockets of rose-fragranced air. When we think of angels appearing, there is a tendency to think of archangels or guardian angels for our protection. In fact, however, it is the pure energy of divine creative thought that touches our soul – beyond categories and beyond words. When we call upon our guardian angels for help in some way, such as healing, comfort, protection or abundance, we open our hearts and minds to this higher vibrational form. We become calmer, more focussed and, very often, this expands to include our family and the area around us.

By concentrating our thoughts on creating the image of an angel, in whatever form, or by meditating on such an image, we are actually connecting to this high vibrational divine energy for ourselves. It is very effective and powerful, and more and more people are learning about – and tapping into – this amazing creative source. When we are working with the angelic realms in an atmosphere of cooperation, this not only lifts our own mood but also helps to generate a profound, almost tangible, change in the atmosphere, wherever we are. In group activity, the change not only affects those taking part but ripples outward like water when a pebble is thrown into a pond. For example, parents making these wonderful origami angels with their children would be establishing a loving, peaceful feeling within the room, which would spread throughout the home. Do make these paper angels in a creative, fun-loving spirit so that they can bring their special charm into your home or place of work. What a joyful way to spread a little heaven!

Chrissie Astell

The Spirit of Origami

For many centuries origami has played a central part in traditional Japanese ceremonies of life and death, from birth rites to weddings to funerals. From the late 6th century, when paper was first introduced into Japan, Shinto priests were fascinated by the beauty, purity and perfection of this material. These qualities were attributed to the gods, so the folding of paper became symbolic of both prayer and offering.

In the West, paper has a more prosaic history, connected with the storage and distribution of knowledge rather than with any spiritual association. However, as we in the modern world look increasingly for spiritual enlightenment, the practice of *origami* (from *ori*, meaning "folding", and *kami*, meaning "paper") has found many adherents who believe there is more to the art than mechanical skill. They strive toward a perfection based on capturing the spirit of the subject with minimal creases, rather than a quest for technological complexity.

The late Japanese Master Akira Yoshizawa, known as the father of contemporary origami, produced clear instructions for folding some of his creations. Yet it's widely acknowledged that few people can even come close to imbuing the models he folded with the same spirit that he gave them. In his youth, Yoshizawa had studied to be a Buddhist priest. Before he folded he would pray and strive to understand the spirit of the creature he was about to create. Many folders see a link between origami and

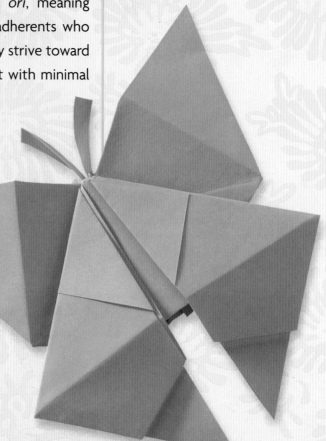

WEDDING SYMBOLISM
In Japan, a crane (opposite) is seen as a bringer of happiness; traditionally, 1,000 paper cranes are given as a wedding gift to represent 1,000 years of married bliss. An origami butterfly (below) is a symbol for the bride or groom.

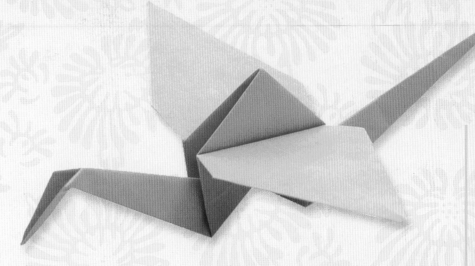

the Buddhist principles of Zen. Origami is a meditative process; the folder becomes "lost" in the paper as he or she strives to shape it. Time stands still and the stresses of everyday life are diminished. The process of folding acts like the repeated words of a mantra, freeing our spirit. The late Eric Kenneway wrote, "the oneness of the square of paper (which has the capacity to become all creatures, interdependent because the square always remains a square) symbolizes their belief in the harmony of the universe and the presence of the Buddha-nature in all things."

An origami designer finds that each original model reaches a point where it seems "complete", when adding further folds would diminish its effectiveness. Thus designers who seek perfection question the addition of every crease – if the original square is the "purest" of states, a great model will work with the paper organically, without superfluous creases. Some believe that the model already lies dormant within the paper, simply awaiting an enlightened folder to liberate it. And so the classic origami models are discovered rather than created. When you follow the steps of this kind of design, you really feel that the artwork you are shaping was "meant to be". It is hugely satisfying to breathe life into an origami model, to give it a spirit that can be sensed by you and others.

TIP: IMPROVISATION

The purist approach to origami angels can produce beautiful creations that are almost works of art. Yet sometimes you might yearn to give your imagination free rein. Simple appliqué can be very appealing. For example, you could use beads, fake pearls, tinsel, or curtain rings (as haloes). This may all be a long way from Japanese tradition, but when you are working for yourself, there are no stylistic taboos. Just see where your instinct takes you.

The Art of Paper Folding

How to use this book

Origami is the art of making models from sheets of paper, ideally with no use of scissors or glue. A simple set of internationally accepted symbols is all you need to understand the diagrams in this book, although you will certainly need to study and practise for the more complicated designs. Some will find paper-folding easier than others, but anyone can do it with a bit of dedication.

This book is intended as a collection of beautiful origami angels rather than a book on origami technique. However, if you work through the designs in the suggested order, you will build up all the skills you need to tackle most origami projects. Always fold each project several times – each new version will be more refined and elegant. Some may take several attempts to get right. By their nature, angels are ethereal creatures, so you are encouraged throughout to experiment with the designs so that they are as expressive as possible. Try to curve the wings and make the models 3D, for example.

How to fold

It's safe to say that if you rush origami, it will show in the results. So, please try to be patient at all times and to fold as slowly and neatly as you can. If possible, arrange to fold in a quiet, clean environment, with decent lighting and few distractions. The act of folding can then become a meditative state and you will feel relaxed and refreshed afterwards.

When learning a new design, fold, unfold and refold each step a few times, so you are clear what is happening and

CREATIVE CARDS
While there is huge satisfaction in making an origami design for its own sake, you can also use many of them as original and unusual cards. For example, the project below (see page 56) makes a wonderful Valentine's card.

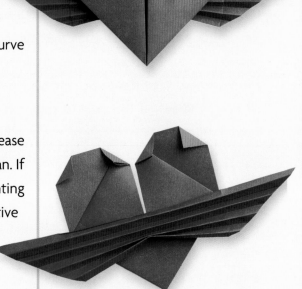

what the diagrams are trying to explain. When the model is complete, make it again at least twice – each time your results will improve. Only you can decide what standard to aim for, so be patient and set your sights high!

Following the diagrams

The instructions in this book consist of two elements – artwork and text. While an experienced folder will not need the text very often, a beginner is encouraged to use every available hint. A suggested method could be:

• Look at the artwork step

• Read the text

• Imagine the result of the fold

• Look at the next artwork step to see how it will develop

• Make the fold, slowly and carefully

If you are keen to refine your skills, repeatedly undo and redo the fold, seeing how the paper is moving and how the artwork is trying to illustrate this. Being able to predict what each step will result in allows you to make a much more precise fold. You will improve with practice.

If you find you cannot complete a model, put it to one side and try again the next day. With complex models, it may take several attempts to achieve a decent standard – as with most manual skills, there is no shortcut to folding ability.

Think creatively at all times – if you want to depart from the given sequence to try and experiment, go for it. You can always return to the instructions later. Many creative giants began by modifying existing work.

CHOOSING PAPER
There is a seemingly endless range of different types of paper to be found these days. Each type may suit one design but not another. The thickness will play a part, as will the texture and strength of the fibre. A good tactic is to build up a collection of as many different sheets as you can buy from various sources; a craft shop, a florist, a stationer's. You will soon learn to gauge how well a given sheet will work, simply by folding it and feeling it. Try thick paper, try thin. As well as paper type, there are myriad colours and patterns to be found. Experiment freely to see which designs look best with which paper.

Basic folds and techniques

The graphic conventions explained below allow folders to make designs even if the instruction text is in another language. This is one of the reasons why origami has such international appeal. After a while, you will need to refer to the written words only occasionally. You may find subtle differences between one book and the next, but the basic set of symbols is pretty consistent.

VALLEY FOLD   Following the arrow, make a fold away from you.

FOLD AND UNFOLD   Fold from the hollow to the solid arrowheads, then unfold

MOUNTAIN FOLD   The paper is folded behind or underneath. You can often turn the paper over and make this as a valley crease.

OPEN OUT / UNFOLD   A wide, hollow arrow is a flexible symbol and indicates paper is either pulled out or unfolded.

REPEAT STEPS   To save time and effort, any steps that are repeated are indicated by an arrow with a short line through the stem. It will tell you which steps to repeat and/or how many times to repeat a single move.

PUSH THE PAPER   A small black triangle indicates that you should press part of the paper, often to encourage a flap or point to fold slightly against its will.

ROTATE PAPER   This symbol tells you to rotate the paper in the direction of the arrows. It might indicate a 90 or 180 degree turn, or even an arbitrary amount – you judge by looking at the next step.

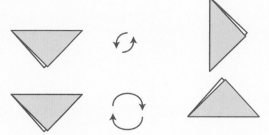

TURN THE PAPER OVER   Lift the paper up and turn it over from side to side.

OUTSIDE REVERSE FOLD   The paper is pre-creased in step 1, then wrapped outside itself in step 2, producing step 3.

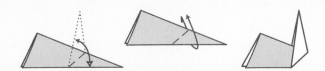

INSIDE REVERSE FOLD   The paper is folded inside other layers, so it is the opposite of the outside reverse. Here are two different applications of the move, on a point and on a corner.

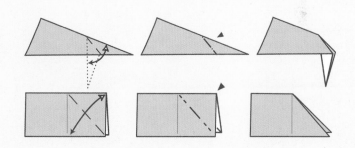

SQUASH FOLD   Generally, an edge is lifted up and squashed symmetrically in half. This move can be pre-creased (so all necessary creases are in place) or just made directly into the paper.

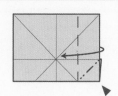
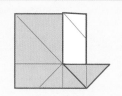

Angels at Home

Fill your home with these delightful angels
and you will enjoy their calming presence
as you go about your daily activities.
From pretty table place cards to wonderful
bookmarks and letters, these angels will make
your home a place of peace and joy.

Bad Hair Angel

Bad hair days will be a thing of the past with this angel on your dressing table, drawing all the bad hair energy away from your head.

"The reason angels can fly is because they take themselves lightly."

G. K. CHESTERTON
(1874–1936)

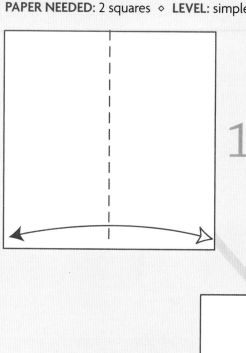

1 Start white side upward, crease in half from side to side, then open.

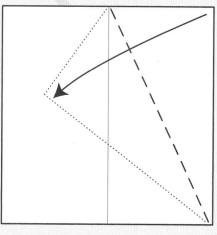

2 Make a fold between the top middle and bottom right.

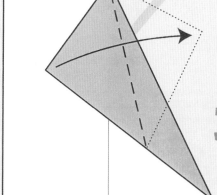

3 Fold the corner back to match the dotted line.

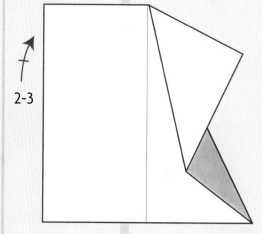

4 Repeat steps 2-3 on the left side.

2-3

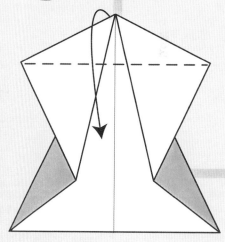

5 Fold the top corner down between the wide points.

6 This is the result.
Turn the paper over.

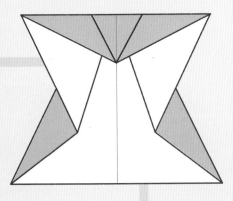

7 This is the body. You will need a new square for the head.

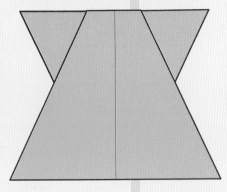

1 Coloured side upwards, crease and unfold both diagonals.

2 Fold the lower edges to the vertical centre, but only make a small pinch where shown.

3 Turn the paper over and rotate to this position. Fold the lower and right edges in to touch where the pinch mark meets the diagonal crease and unfold. Repeat with the other two sides.

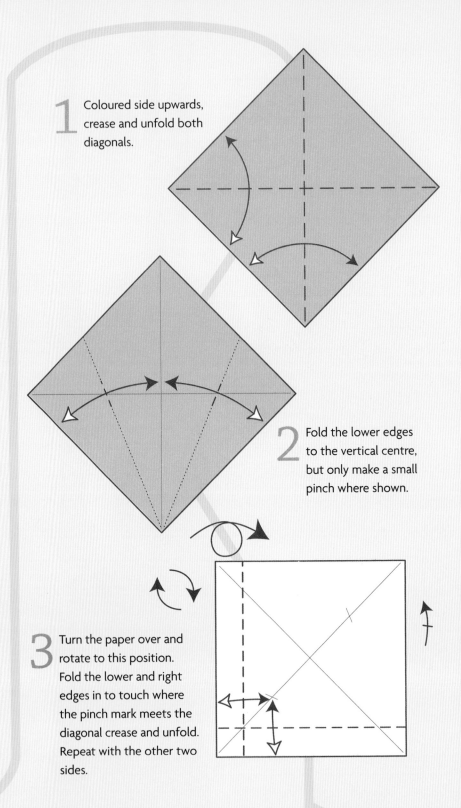

4 Fold side to opposite side, crease and unfold in both directions.

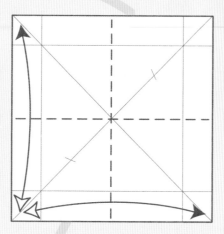

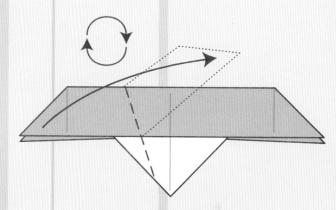

5 Collapse using these creases – the only ones that need changing are the outer ends of the diagonals, change these to valleys.

7 Fold the first corner on the left to match the dotted line.

6 Here is the result. Rotate the paper 180 degrees.

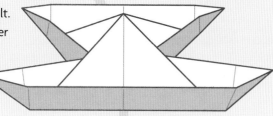

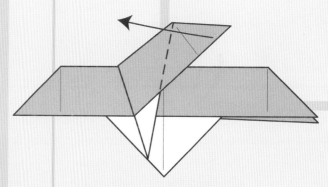

8 Fold the corner back along the edge underneath.

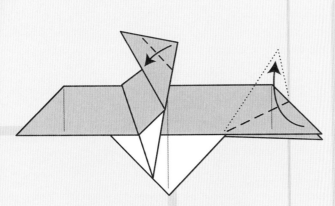

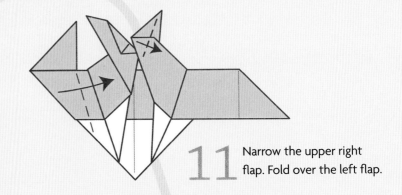

9 Fold the right corner to match the dotted line. Narrow the flap on the left.

11 Narrow the upper right flap. Fold over the left flap.

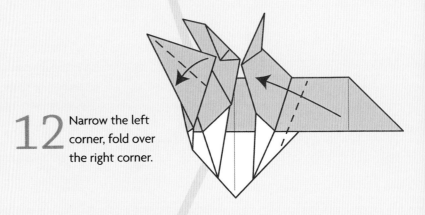

12 Narrow the left corner, fold over the right corner.

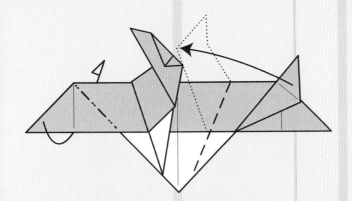

10 Fold the right flap to match the dotted line. Fold the flap on the left underneath.

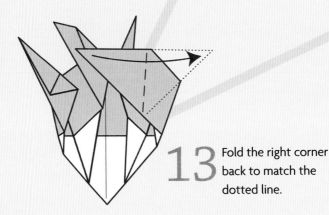

13 Fold the right corner back to match the dotted line.

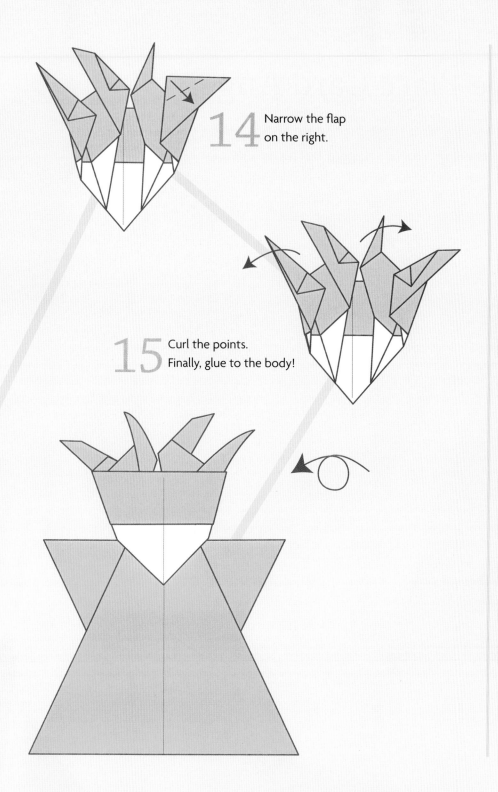

14 Narrow the flap on the right.

15 Curl the points. Finally, glue to the body!

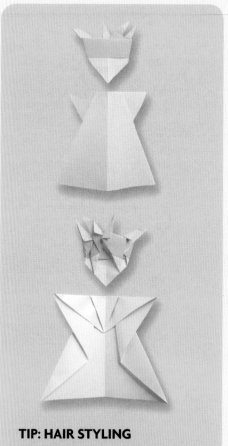

TIP: HAIR STYLING

When folding the strands of hair, have a look at the model from the front before finally flattening the fold. This will give you a better idea of how the final result will look.

The sequence shown to create the hair is only a suggestion, you should experiment to create different hair arrangements. Another possibility is to create two different heads and slide one inside the other to double the amount of hair. Really creative folders might wish to try to attach the head without glue!

Table Place Card Angel

Make dinner parties extra-special with these place card angels. Write your guest's name on the body of the angel for an elegant butterfly-like place card.

"Do not forget to entertain strangers, for by so doing some have unwittingly entertained angels."

THE BIBLE
(HEBREWS 13:2)

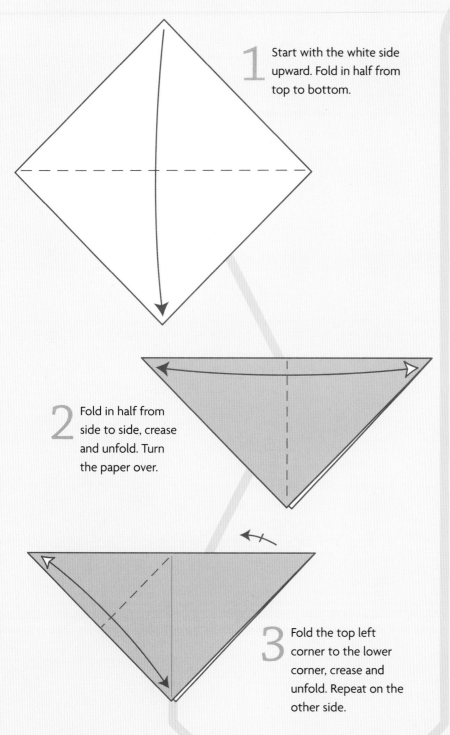

1 Start with the white side upward. Fold in half from top to bottom.

2 Fold in half from side to side, crease and unfold. Turn the paper over.

3 Fold the top left corner to the lower corner, crease and unfold. Repeat on the other side.

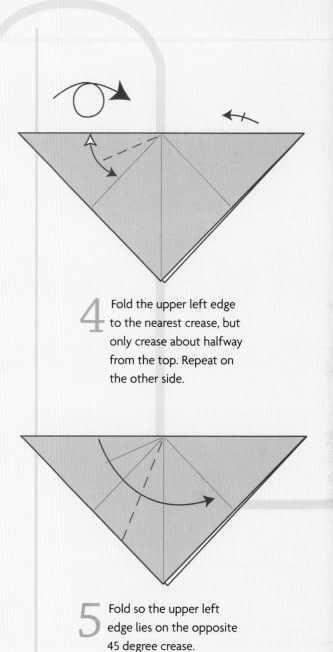

4 Fold the upper left edge to the nearest crease, but only crease about halfway from the top. Repeat on the other side.

5 Fold so the upper left edge lies on the opposite 45 degree crease.

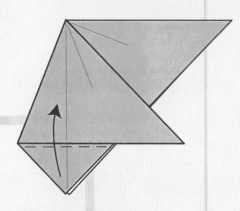

6 Fold the lower corners over the horizontal edge.

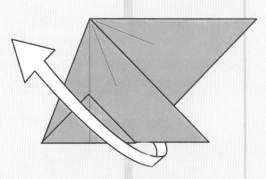

7 Unfold the flap to the right, leaving the last step in place.

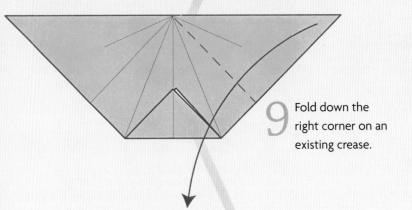

8 Fold the lower right edge to lie on the bottom edge, crease and unfold.

9 Fold down the right corner on an existing crease.

10 Fold it back up to match the dotted line. The crease starts at the top of the small triangle and the upper edge meets the top right edge at a right angle.

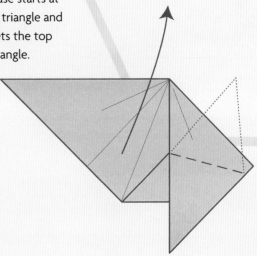

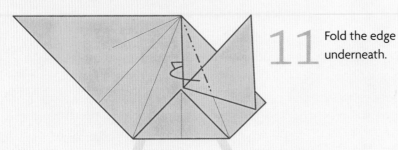

11 Fold the edge underneath.

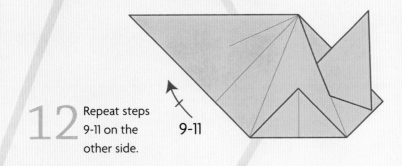

12 Repeat steps 9-11 on the other side.

9-11

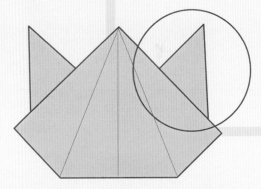

14 We now focus on the circled area.

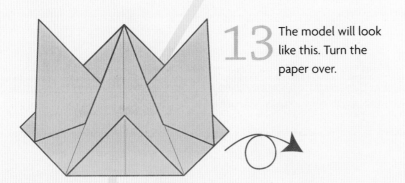

13 The model will look like this. Turn the paper over.

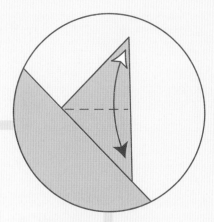

15 Fold the triangle in half, crease and unfold.

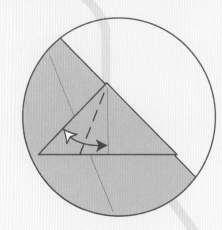

17 Fold so the upper edge meets the crease, then unfold.

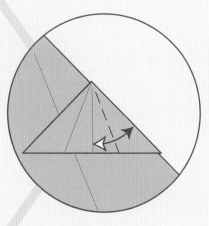

18 Fold so the crease from the right-angled corner lies on the outer edge. Crease and unfold.

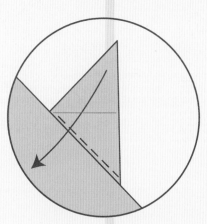

16 Fold the triangle over the folded edge.

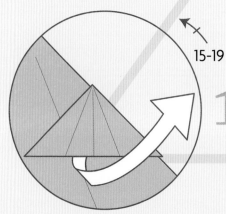

15-19

19 Unfold the wing and repeat steps 15-19 on the other wing.

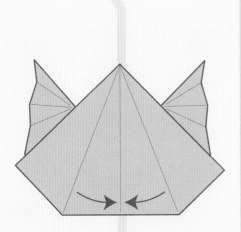

20 Form into 3D using these creases.

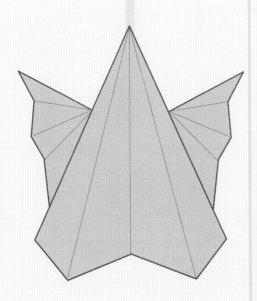

TIP: CRISP CREASES

One of the key features of this design is that it is strongly three-dimensional. This is best achieved by using crisp paper and making your creases nice and sharp. Try not to fold and unfold too often, since this weakens the creases and makes it hard to create the well-defined angles shown in the photo.

Steps 15-18 show the easiest configuration of wing creases, but feel free to alter these if you wish.

Bookmark Angel

A handy little angel to keep your place in the latest book you're reading –
make several of them if you have a few books on the go.

*"An angel can illuminate the
thought and mind of man by
strengthening the power of vision."*

ST THOMAS AQUINAS
(1225–1274)

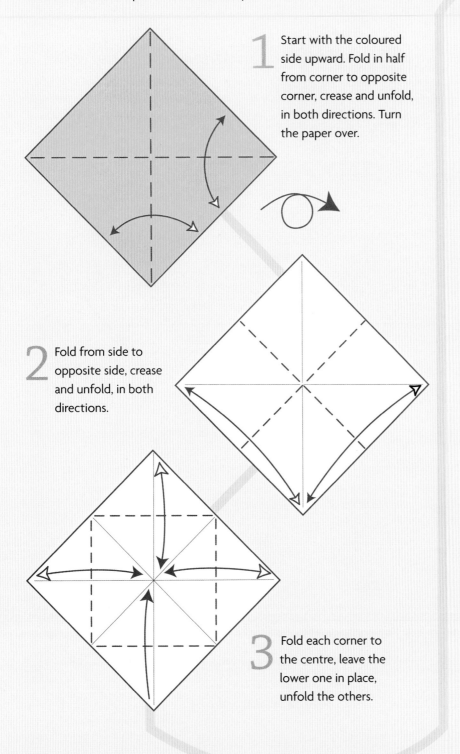

1 Start with the coloured side upward. Fold in half from corner to opposite corner, crease and unfold, in both directions. Turn the paper over.

2 Fold from side to opposite side, crease and unfold, in both directions.

3 Fold each corner to the centre, leave the lower one in place, unfold the others.

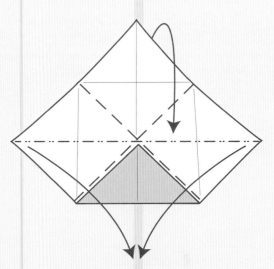

4 Collapse the paper down on existing creases.

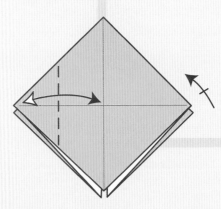

5 Fold the left corner to the centre, crease and unfold. Repeat on the right.

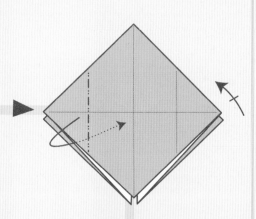

6 Reverse the corner inside. Repeat on the right. (See tip.)

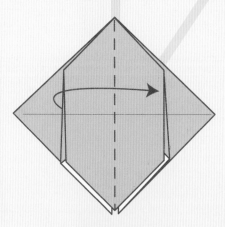

7 Fold a flap from left to right, as shown.

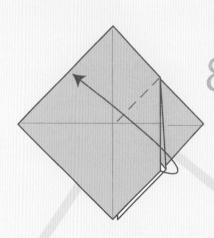

8 Partially unfold a flap, as shown.

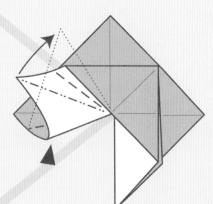

9 Fold the white corner (made with a diagonal) to match the dotted line, flatten the paper into position. (See tip.)

10 Tuck the end of the flap inside.

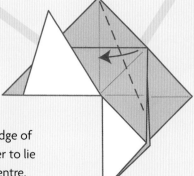

11 Fold the upper edge of the right flap over to lie on the vertical centre.

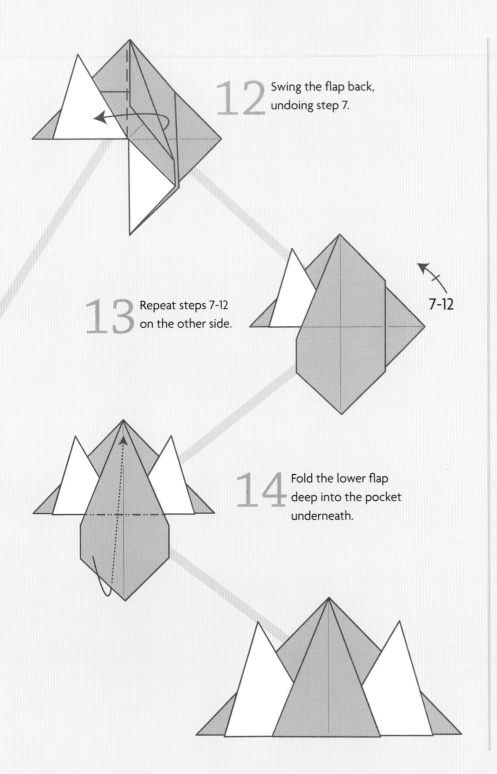

12 Swing the flap back, undoing step 7.

13 Repeat steps 7-12 on the other side.

7-12

14 Fold the lower flap deep into the pocket underneath.

TIP: STAYING ACCURATE

The "reverse fold" in step 6 can confuse the beginner. The key is to make a sharp, accurate crease in the previous step, then open the layers slightly and press the outer corner so it folds inside, sitting in between the layers.

Step 9 is known as a "swivel" in the world of origami. If you fold the mountain crease that extends to the white corner, then position the corner where you want it to be, you can gently press the rest of the paper flat to form the other creases.

Angel Letter

Write your letter on one side of the paper and then fold up the sheet to form an angelic messenger whom you can address and stamp and post to a friend.

" If instead of a gem, or even a flower, we should cast the gift of a loving thought into the heart of a friend, that would be giving as the angels give."

GEORGE MACDONALD
(1824–1905)

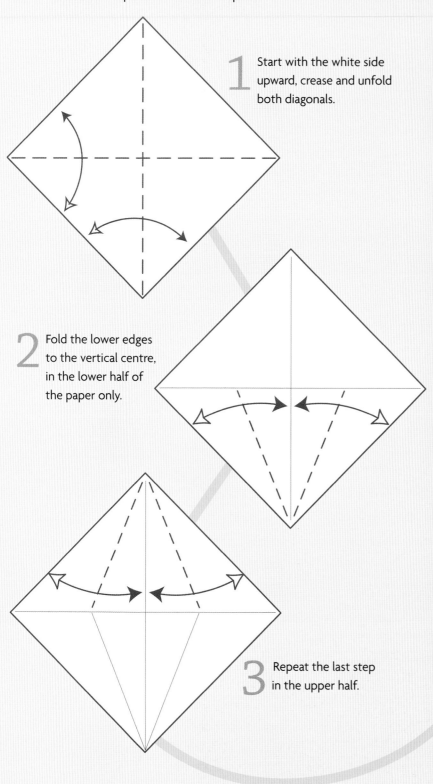

1 Start with the white side upward, crease and unfold both diagonals.

2 Fold the lower edges to the vertical centre, in the lower half of the paper only.

3 Repeat the last step in the upper half.

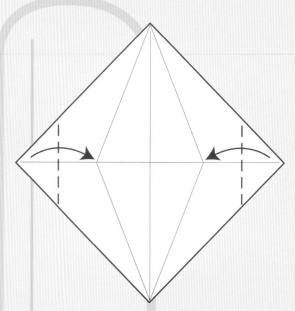

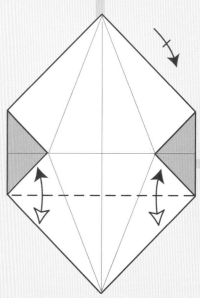

4 Fold the outer corners to the crease intersections.

5 Fold the lower corner up so the edges lie on the edges formed in the last step. Crease and unfold. Repeat the move on the upper half.

6 Fold so the lower edges meet the horizontal crease, but only extend these creases where shown.

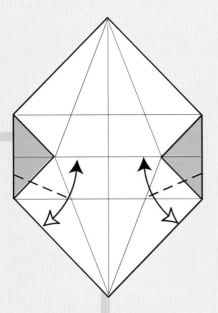

7 Fold on the (existing) valley creases, forming the new mountain creases as you collapse the paper upward. (See tip, page 37.)

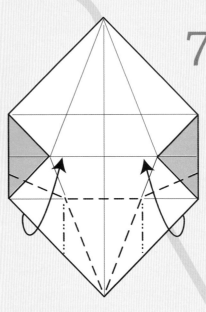

8 Fold the tip of the pointed flap over to match a crease on the layer underneath.

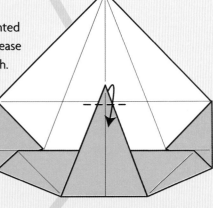

9 Fold the same flap underneath to form a straight horizontal edge.

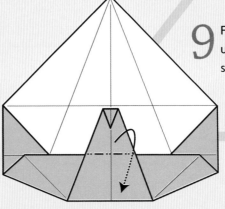

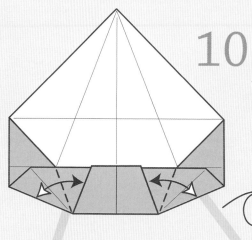

10 Fold the lower, outer edges to meet the edge of the flap just tucked inside. Crease only where shown, then unfold. Turn the paper over. (See tip, page 37.)

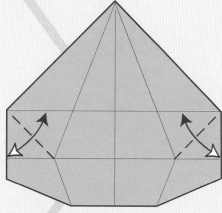

11 Fold the vertical edges to the horizontal crease, creasing only where shown, then unfold.

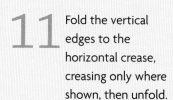

12 Turn the paper over from top to bottom. Use these (existing) creases to collapse the paper inwards.

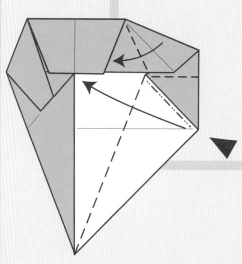

13 Repeat the last step on the right.

14 Fold the lower flap upward – the crease is already in place on the lower layer.

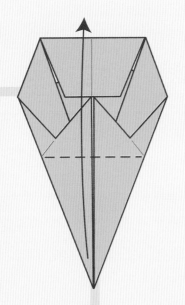

15 Fold the top flap over the edge (pull it slightly up when doing so).

16 Unfold the flap.

17 Refold the flap, tucking it into the pocket.

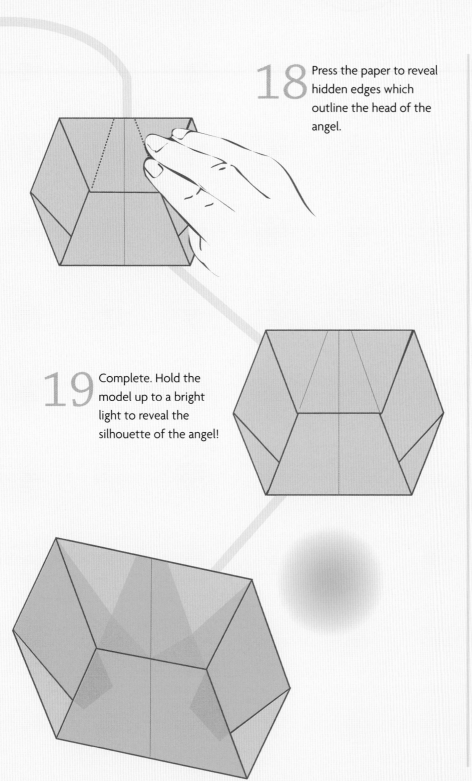

18 Press the paper to reveal hidden edges which outline the head of the angel.

19 Complete. Hold the model up to a bright light to reveal the silhouette of the angel!

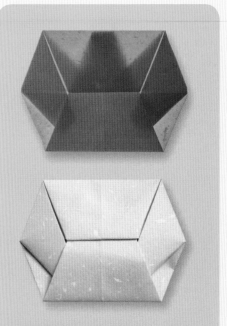

TIP: FREESTYLE FOLD

Step 7 is one of the few folds in the book where not all the creases are put in place before the fold. Nevertheless, it is not difficult if you let the paper do the work for you. Simply fold the flap upwards along the valley creases and, as the paper begins to flatten, allow it to settle where it will, then carefully flatten the paper to form the mountain creases you need.

The creases in steps 10 and 11 allow you to complete the collapse in step 13, so make them carefully and firmly, since you are creasing through several layers at that stage.

In order to see the silhouette properly, fold with thinner paper than usual, or use a very bright light!

Gift Box Angel

Make sure your gift box is as lovely as the sparkly present within it.
Here is a charming angel box with wings to carry your special gift to that special person.

*" Angels knew from the very start
that the gifts of love
are gifts of the heart."*

ANONYMOUS

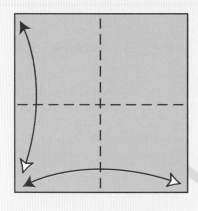

1 Coloured side upward, fold in half, then unfold, in both directions.

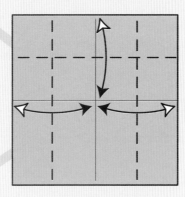

2 Add quarter creases on three sides.

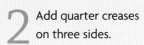

3 Fold the lower right corner to the opposite ¾ point, crease where shown, then unfold.

4 Turn the paper over. Crease both diagonals.

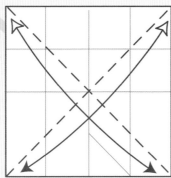

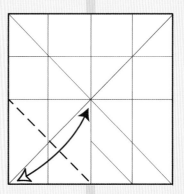

5 Fold the bottom left corner to the centre, crease and unfold.

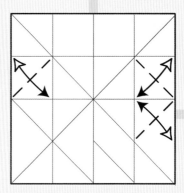

6 Add three more short valley creases where shown.

7 Fold the lower edge to the centre.

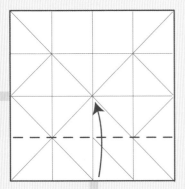

8 This is the result. Turn the paper over.

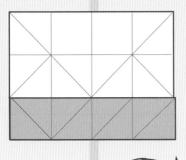

9 Reinforce these two crease as valleys.

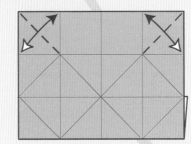

10 Fold the right side inward, squashing the lower corner into a triangle.

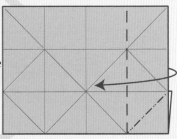

11 This is the result. Repeat on the other side.

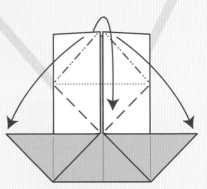

12 Fold the corners at the top down and out, squashing the paper on existing creases. Check the next step for guidance.

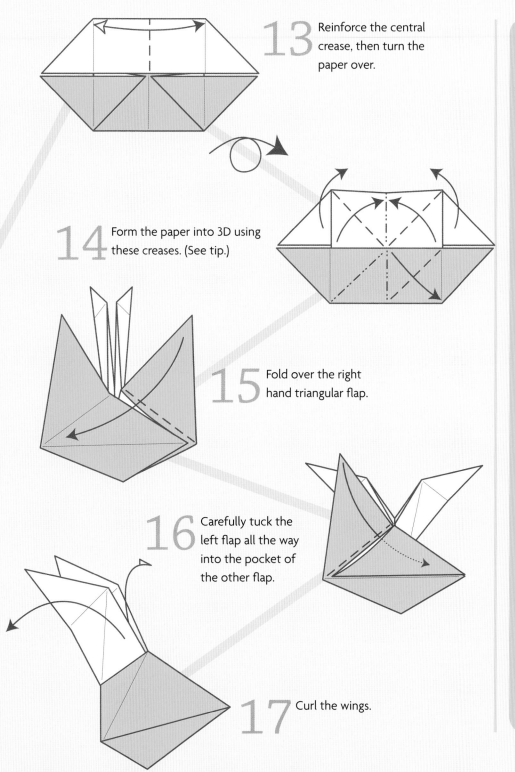

13 Reinforce the central crease, then turn the paper over.

14 Form the paper into 3D using these creases. (See tip.)

15 Fold over the right hand triangular flap.

16 Carefully tuck the left flap all the way into the pocket of the other flap.

17 Curl the wings.

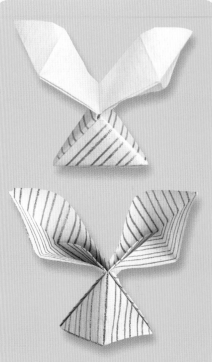

TIP: FIDDLY CREASES

Step 14 is hard to visualize, but if you use the existing creases, it will (almost!) form itself. The shape you are trying to achieve is an irregular hexagon, formed of six right-angled triangles – think of it as two three-sided pyramids joined together at their bases. Take your time – the creases are already there. Gently encourage them into place, forming the paper into 3D. At no time try to introduce any new creases, or force the paper: you are simply readjusting the relative positions of the flaps. The white flaps (which are the wings) swing back out of the way.

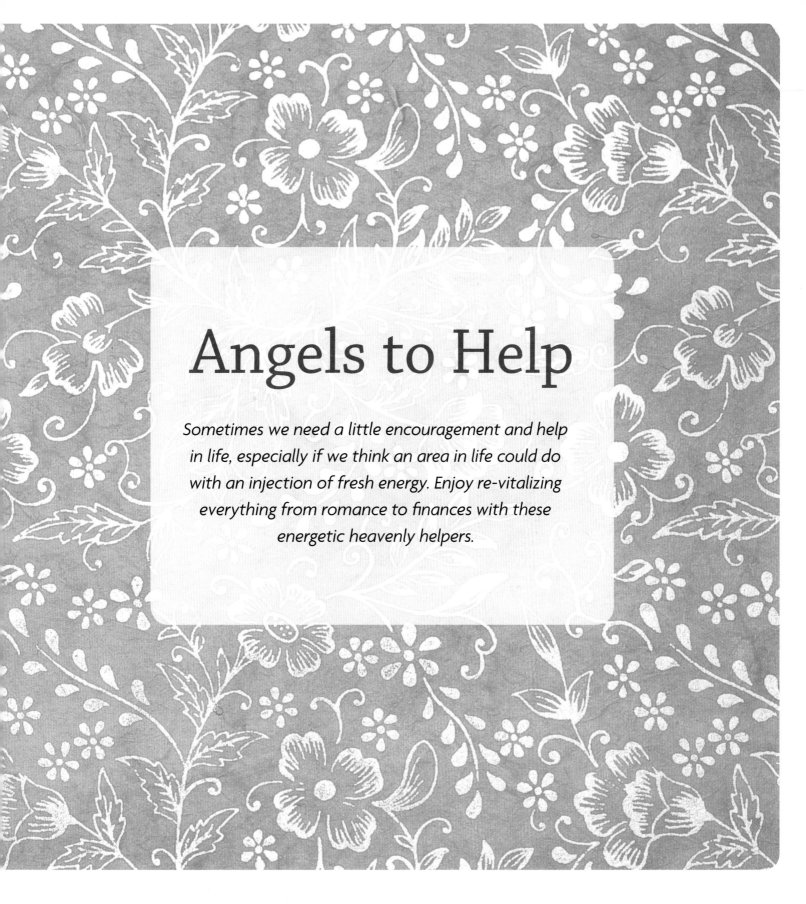

Angels to Help

Sometimes we need a little encouragement and help in life, especially if we think an area in life could do with an injection of fresh energy. Enjoy re-vitalizing everything from romance to finances with these energetic heavenly helpers.

Good Luck Angel

Sometimes you need a little extra luck in life, whether it's having the confidence to pursue and win that dream job or getting the right questions so that you can pass that exam with flying colours. Focus on your success while you're making this little fellow and wish yourself an extra dash of good fortune.

" Make friends with the angels, who though invisible are always with you. Often invoke them, constantly praise them, and make good use of their help and assistance in all your temporal and spiritual affairs."

ST FRANCIS DE SALES
(1567–1622)

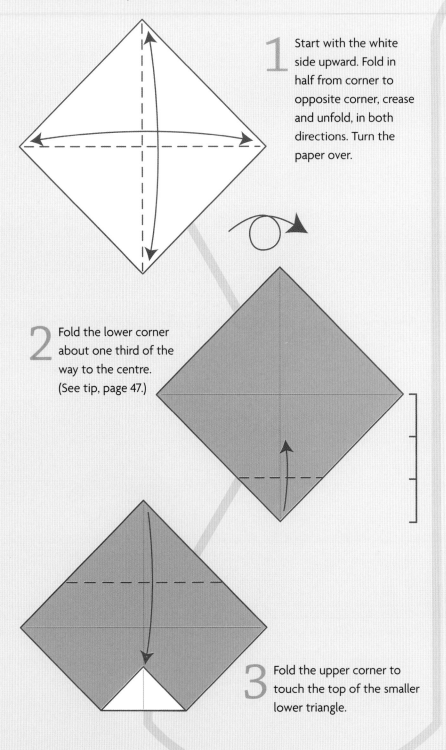

1 Start with the white side upward. Fold in half from corner to opposite corner, crease and unfold, in both directions. Turn the paper over.

2 Fold the lower corner about one third of the way to the centre. (See tip, page 47.)

3 Fold the upper corner to touch the top of the smaller lower triangle.

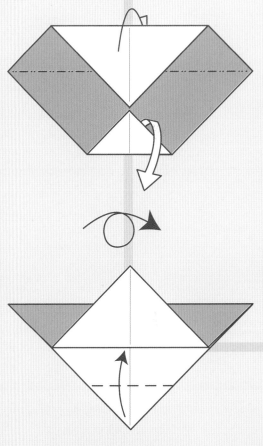

4 Unfold the lower corner, fold the upper section behind on the diagonal. Turn the paper over.

5 Fold the lower corner upwards by reversing an existing crease.

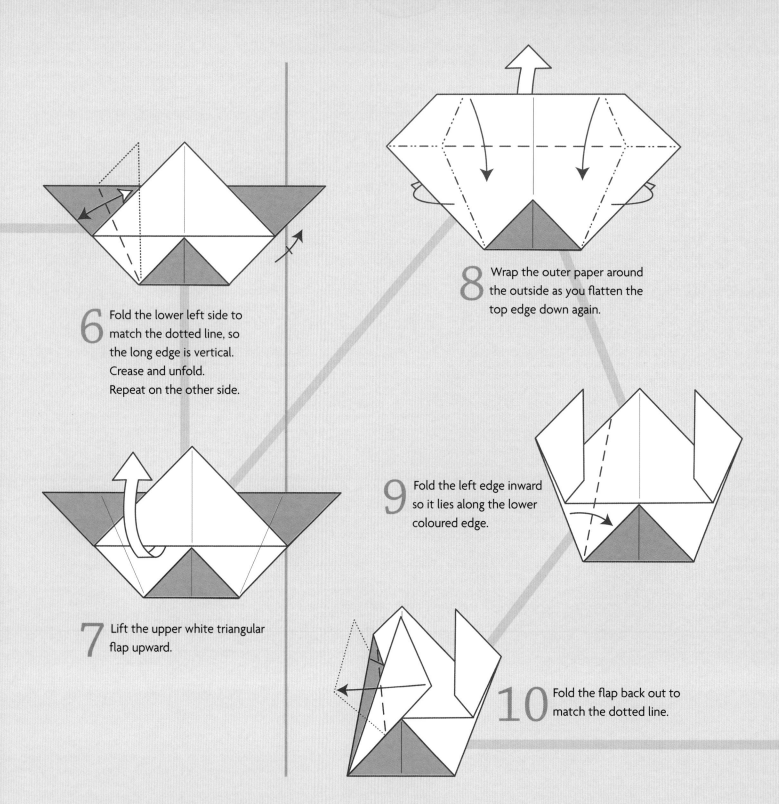

6 Fold the lower left side to match the dotted line, so the long edge is vertical. Crease and unfold. Repeat on the other side.

7 Lift the upper white triangular flap upward.

8 Wrap the outer paper around the outside as you flatten the top edge down again.

9 Fold the left edge inward so it lies along the lower coloured edge.

10 Fold the flap back out to match the dotted line.

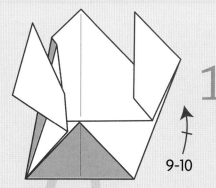

11

Repeat steps 9-10 on the right. (It may help to fold the model in half to make sure the wings match up before flattening.)

9-10

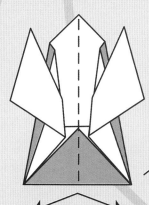

12

Reinforce the central crease so the model will stand. Turn the model over.

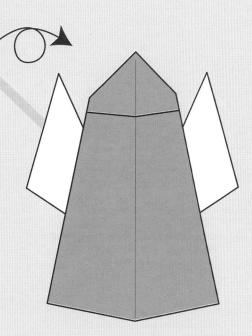

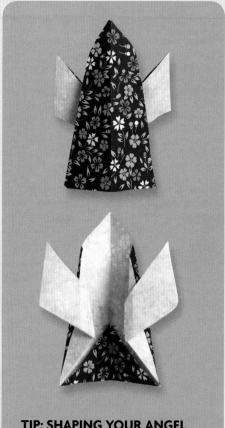

TIP: SHAPING YOUR ANGEL

The overall proportions of this design are determined by the fold in step 2. Try making this fold shorter or longer and see how it affects the final model. Many creative possibilities exist in origami when you adjust distances or angles. Sometimes it works, sometimes it ruins the design, but by trying, you are following the same creative journey that the designer went through when they made their decisions for the prototype.

Angel of Communication

This angelic helper will make all your calls run smoothly and ensure your letters and emails are well received. Try making it in blue, traditionally the colour of communication, and then focus on its elegant wings for a while before making that important contact.

"Angels can hear a whisper in a whirlwind; and when they answer, you will find their healing wisdom in the echo-chamber of your soul."

ANONYMOUS PRAYER FROM PORTUGAL

1 Start with the white side upward. Fold in half from top to bottom.

2 Fold in half from side to side, crease and unfold.

3 Fold the top left corner to the lower corner.

4 Fold the upper left edge to the vertical centre, then unfold. Repeat steps 3-4 on the other side.

3-4

5 Fold both lower corners upward between the ends of the nearest creases.

6 Pleat the paper inward.

7 Fold the short lower edge to lie on the crease, crease firmly, then unfold.

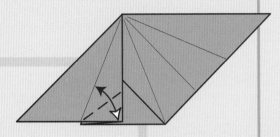

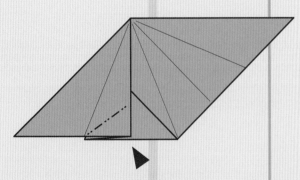

8 Make an inside reverse fold on the recent crease.

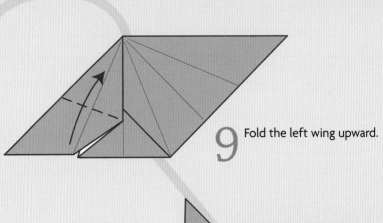

9 Fold the left wing upward.

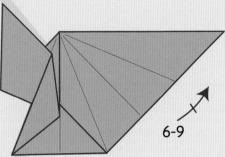

10 This is the result. Repeat steps 6-9 on the other side.

6-9

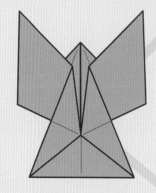

11 This is the result. Turn the paper over.

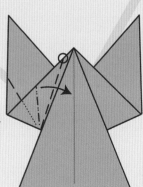

12 Fold a flap inward, the crease ends slightly away from the top corner (circled). Press flat to flatten the wing. (See tip.)

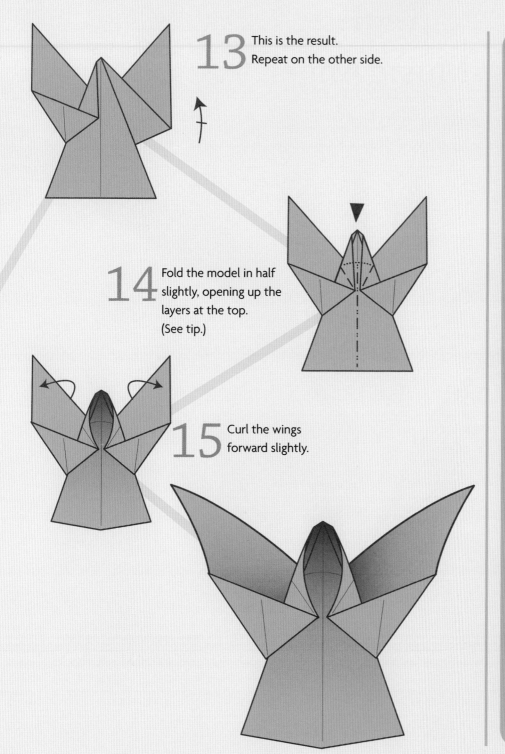

13 This is the result. Repeat on the other side.

14 Fold the model in half slightly, opening up the layers at the top. (See tip.)

15 Curl the wings forward slightly.

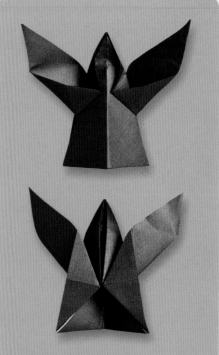

TIP: HANDLE WITH CARE

Step 12 is an example of a "swivel", in origami terms. You are rearranging the position of a flap (the outer one with a folded edge), and to allow the paper to flatten you have to create a new crease on the lower edge of the wing. The move is slightly complicated by the fact that the inner valley crease does not lie along the inner folded edge, but at a slight angle to it. This is to create a slightly more rounded head. If you find this too "fiddly", just fold over the edge.

Step 14, where you open the layers of the head and press inside slightly to round the paper, needs only gentle pressure, so be careful!

Music Angel

Angels have always been associated with celestial music, so this tuneful figure makes a great gift for music lovers – try using sheet music as paper for an unusually apt result.

"Music is well said to be the speech of angels."

THOMAS CARLYLE
(1795–1881)

PAPER NEEDED: 1 triangle ◇ **LEVEL:** intermediate

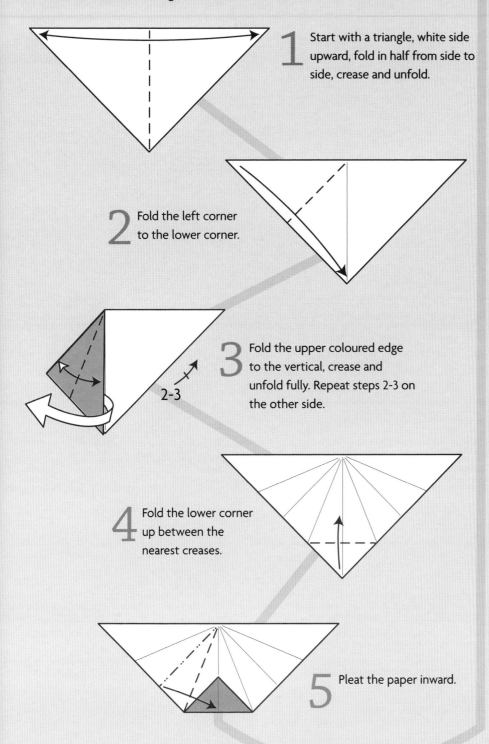

1 Start with a triangle, white side upward, fold in half from side to side, crease and unfold.

2 Fold the left corner to the lower corner.

3 Fold the upper coloured edge to the vertical, crease and unfold fully. Repeat steps 2-3 on the other side.

2-3

4 Fold the lower corner up between the nearest creases.

5 Pleat the paper inward.

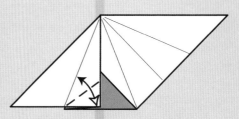

6 Fold the lower edge to the nearest crease, then unfold.

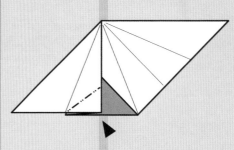

7 Reverse the corner inside.

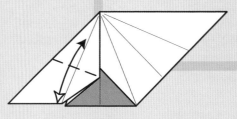

8 Fold the wing upward on a hidden edge.

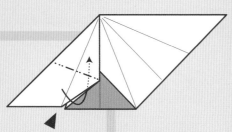

9 Reverse the same wing inside.

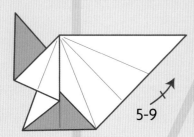

5-9

10 Repeat steps 5-9 on the right side.

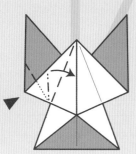

11 Fold the white edge to the vertical centre, squashing the paper to match.

12 This is the result. Repeat on the right side.

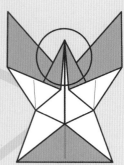

13 The model so far. Now we focus on the circled area.

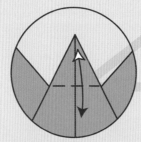

14 Fold the top corner down between the two corners, crease and unfold.

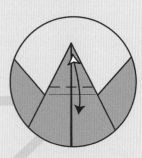

15 Make a similar fold a little way higher.

16 Open the upper layers.

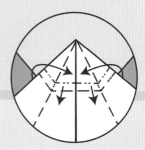

17 Refold the model as you make a pleat all the way around. (See tip.)

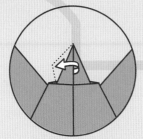

18 Ease out paper to match the dotted line and flatten into the new position.

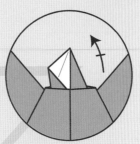

19 Repeat on the right side.

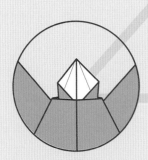

20 This is the result.

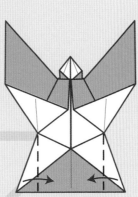

21 Fold the sides of the body in.

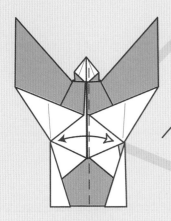

22 Reinforce the central crease so the model will stand.

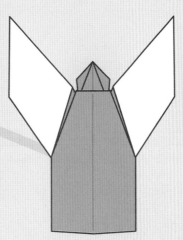

TIP: CONTRASTING WINGS

This design is made from a triangle of paper, formed by folding, then cutting along the diagonal of a square. This allows the reverse side of the paper to form the wings with a contrasting colour. If you prefer, you can fold the model using a square folded along the diagonal. This will produce the same model, although twice as thick and so slightly more tricky to fold, and you will have wings the same colour as the body.

Step 17 can be visualized by looking at step 16 and imagining the tip of the paper "sunk" downward, then partially folded back up.

Love Heart Angel

Whether you use this angel to attract love into your life or make it as a gift for your beloved on Valentine's Day, this angel of the heart is a peaceful symbol of romance.

"Angels have no philosophy but love."

ANONYMOUS, SOURCED BY TERRI GUILLEMETS
(B. 1973)

PAPER NEEDED: 1 square ◇ LEVEL: intermediate

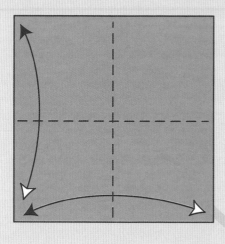

1 Start with the coloured side upwards. Crease from side to opposite side, then unfold, in both directions.

2 Fold the top edge to the centre.

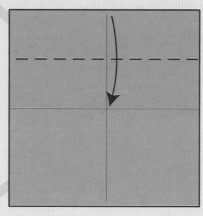

3 This is the result. Turn the paper over.

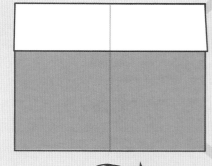

4 Make two small diagonal folds through all layers, then unfold.

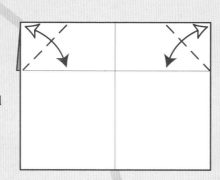

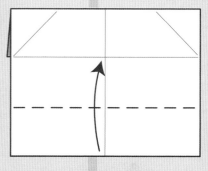

5 Fold the lower edge to the centre.

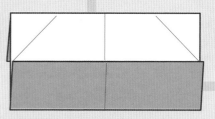

6 This is the result. Turn the paper over.

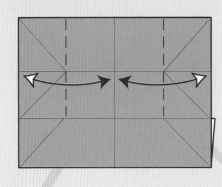

9 Fold the sides to the centre, creasing where shown, then unfold.

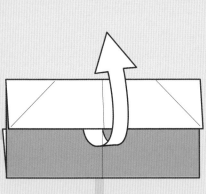

7 Unfold the upper flap.

10 Take two small diagonal folds through all layers, then unfold.

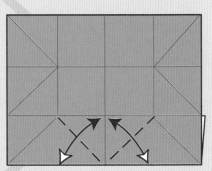

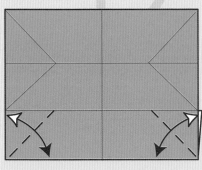

8 Make two diagonal crease through the upper layer only.

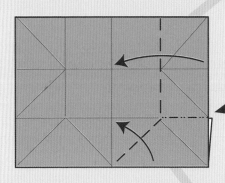

11 Use these (existing) creases to collapse the paper to the left.

12 Repeat the last step on the left.

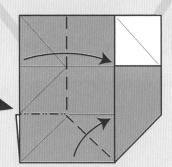

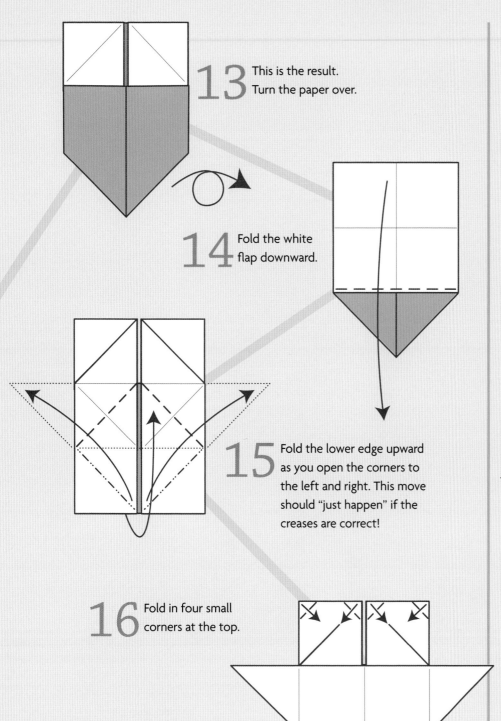

13 This is the result. Turn the paper over.

14 Fold the white flap downward.

15 Fold the lower edge upward as you open the corners to the left and right. This move should "just happen" if the creases are correct!

16 Fold in four small corners at the top.

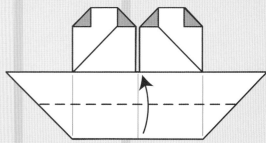

17 Fold the lower flap in half. (See tip, page 61.)

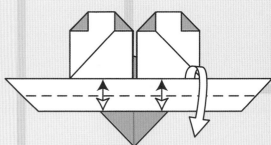

18 Fold the narrow strip in half, crease firmly then unfold the flap fully.

19
Convert all these creases to valleys. Rotate the model 180 degrees.

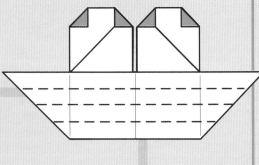

20
Fold the large upper flap downward.

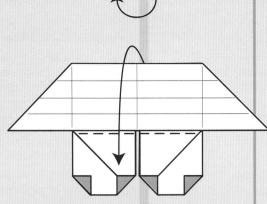

21
Add valley creases halfway between the existing creases. (See tip.)

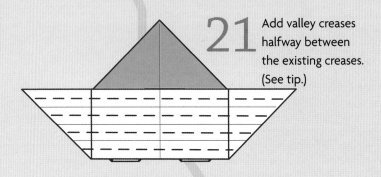

22
Pleat the paper on existing creases. Rotate the model 180 degrees.

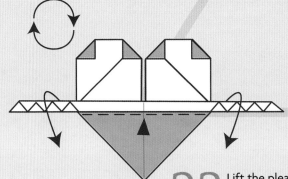

23
Lift the pleats up to half way, press gently in the centre and unfold the edges downward. (See tip.)

23

This is the result.
Turn the paper over.

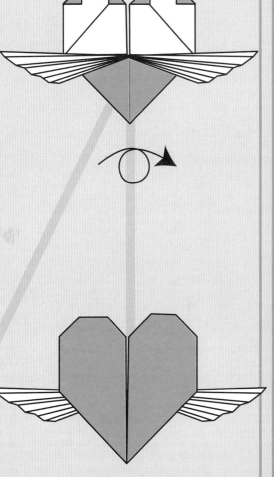

TIP: GETTING DEXTEROUS

The formation of the wings in this design requires folding that is very precise, in order for the final model to look as neat as possible. Take extra care during the creasing at steps 17 and 18 and again at step 21, where you add new creases exactly halfway between the existing creases. With a small starting square, this can be quite demanding, but fold slowly and crease firmly.

Step 23 requires you to try and keep the layers together at the centre, whilst opening them out at either end. This seemingly impossible task can be done with a bit of patience.

Money Angel

When kept beside your piggy bank or popped into your purse or wallet, this angel will help you focus on, and hopefully attract, prosperity and wealth.

"There are people who have money and there are people who are rich."

COCO CHANEL
(1883–1971)

1 Start with a dollar bill or similar banknote. Fold in half, crease and unfold. (See tip.)

2 Fold in half downward.

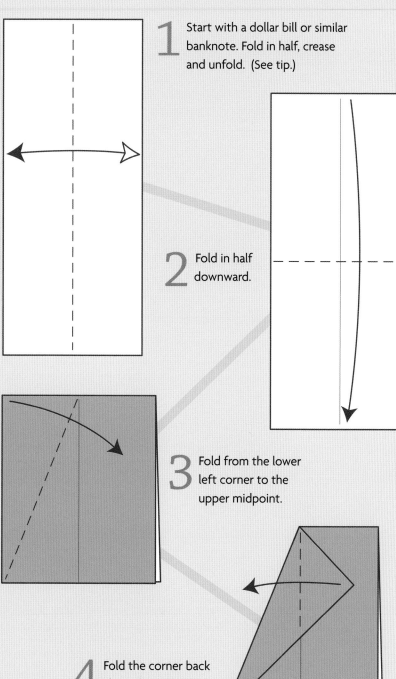

3 Fold from the lower left corner to the upper midpoint.

4 Fold the corner back along the vertical crease underneath.

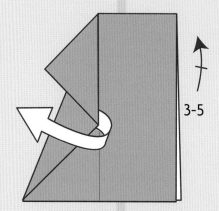

3-5

5 Unfold the last two steps and repeat them on the right side.

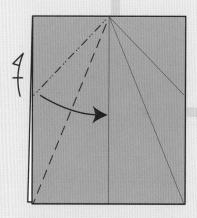

6 Make these folds on both sides at the same time. (See tip, page 65.)

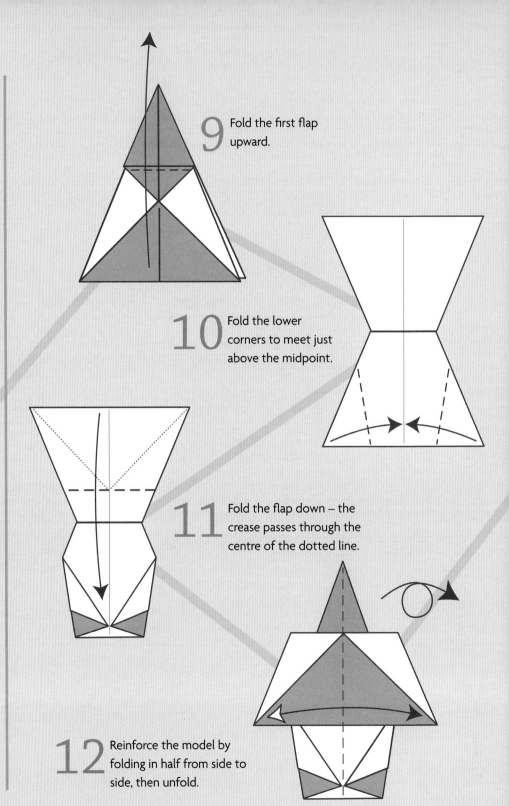

9 Fold the first flap upward.

10 Fold the lower corners to meet just above the midpoint.

11 Fold the flap down – the crease passes through the centre of the dotted line.

12 Reinforce the model by folding in half from side to side, then unfold.

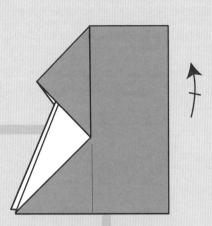

7 This is the result. Repeat on the other side.

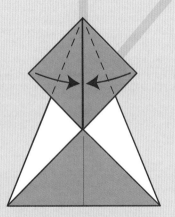

8 Fold the upper edges to the vertical centre.

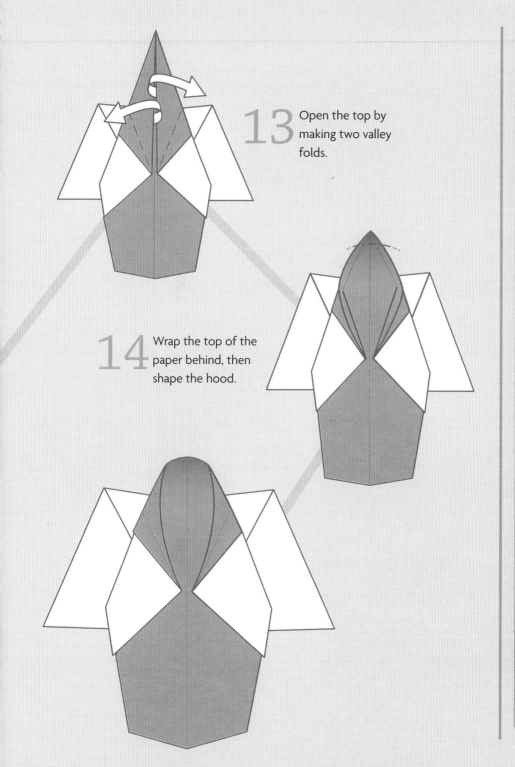

13 Open the top by making two valley folds.

14 Wrap the top of the paper behind, then shape the hood.

TIP: MAKING A DOLLAR

If you don't have a dollar bill lying around, you can create the same shape by cutting a square from an A4 rectangle – the part that is left is the shape we need.

Step 6 has the creases in place, but they will only be correct on one side. On the other side, you will need to convert valley to mountain and vice versa. The move can be done in two steps, but is more fun if you can make it happen in one.

Angels to Inspire

Some angels transcend the everyday, and contemplating their beautiful wings or a prayerful pose can be inspiring and uplifting. Making these angels can give rise to a profound sense of serenity and divine love.

Friendship Angel

This cheery angel will remind you of the power of friendship to dispel gloom and make your burdens lighter. An ideal gift to make for friends to show them how much you care.

"Think where man's glory most begins and ends,
And say my glory was I had such friends."

WILLIAM BUTLER YEATS
(1865–1939)

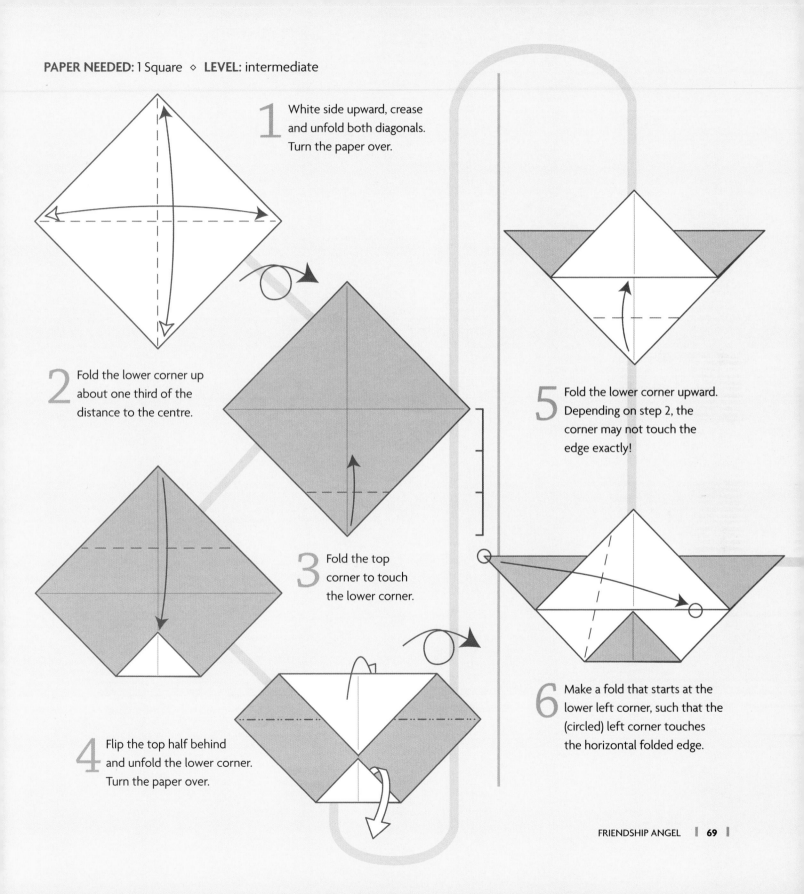

1 White side upward, crease and unfold both diagonals. Turn the paper over.

2 Fold the lower corner up about one third of the distance to the centre.

3 Fold the top corner to touch the lower corner.

4 Flip the top half behind and unfold the lower corner. Turn the paper over.

5 Fold the lower corner upward. Depending on step 2, the corner may not touch the edge exactly!

6 Make a fold that starts at the lower left corner, such that the (circled) left corner touches the horizontal folded edge.

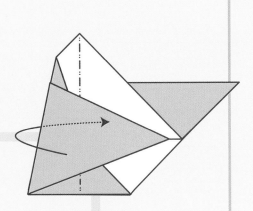

7 Flip the paper behind on the left side.

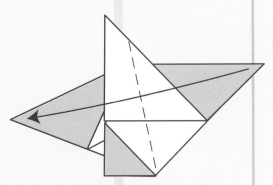

8 Fold the right corner to lie on the matching corner on the left.

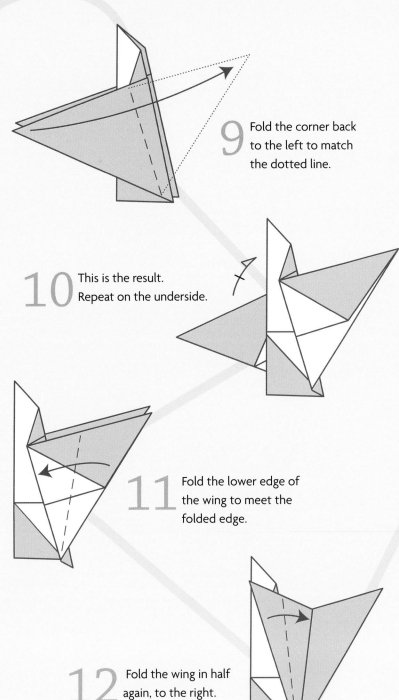

9 Fold the corner back to the left to match the dotted line.

10 This is the result. Repeat on the underside.

11 Fold the lower edge of the wing to meet the folded edge.

12 Fold the wing in half again, to the right.

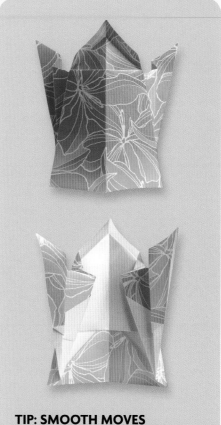

13 This is the result. Repeat steps 9-12 on the underside. (See tip.)

9-12

14 Open the model out evenly.

15 Fold the model in half behind, folding the top of the head forward with small valley folds. (See tip.)

16 Open and shape the wings.

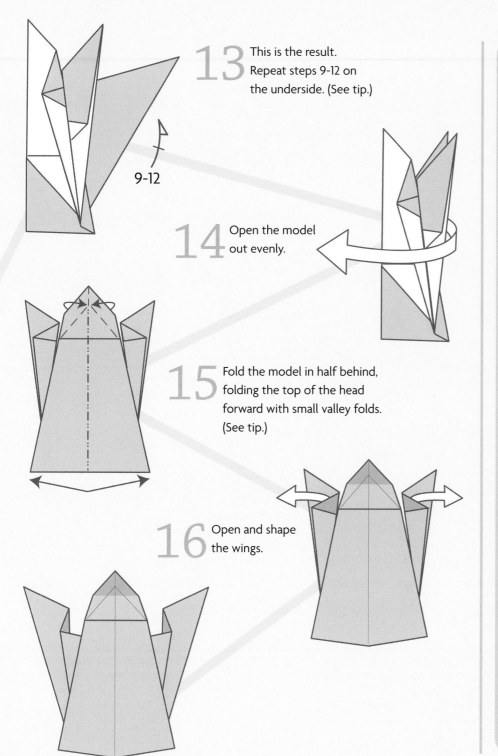

TIP: SMOOTH MOVES

The folding sequence here was chosen to ensure that the wings are symmetrical. You may prefer to work out your own way of folding it – there are always many different ways to achieve the same end result.

At step 13 you can add more pleats to the wings if you wish. There are no reference points for step 15: just ease the paper round so that it faces forward and gives the head a more three-dimensional feel. Make these folds gently so they are smooth rather than sharp creases.

Angel on the Wall

This angel is designed to watch over you and your loved ones, bringing a sense of peace and harmony into your home, whichever room you hang it in.

"We are each of us angels with only one wing, and we can only fly by embracing one another."

LUCIANO DE CRESCENZO
(B. 1928)

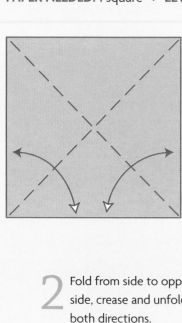

1 Start with the coloured side upward. Fold in half from corner to opposite corner, crease and unfold, in both directions. Turn the paper over.

2 Fold from side to opposite side, crease and unfold, in both directions.

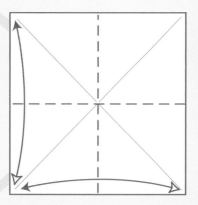

3 Collapse the paper downward using these creases.

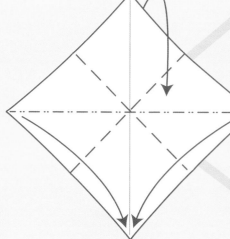

4 Fold the lower edges (upper layers only) to the vertical centre.

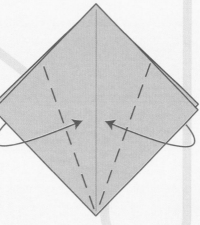

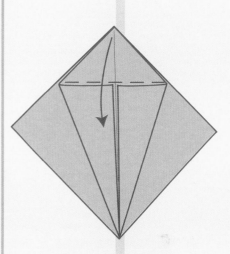

5 Fold the triangular flap over the layers.

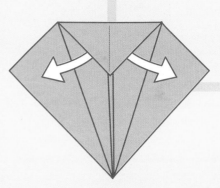

6 Unfold the flaps from step 4.

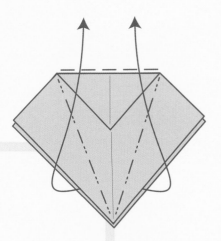

7 Lift up the first layer and swing it upward.

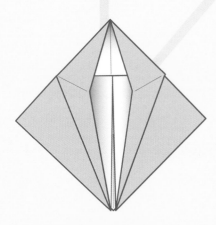

8 The move in progress.

9 Complete. Repeat steps 4-8 on the underside.

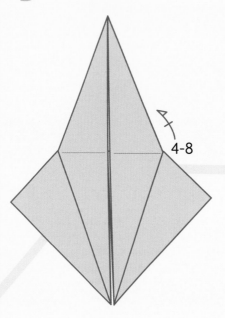

4-8

10 Unfold back to the square on the white side.

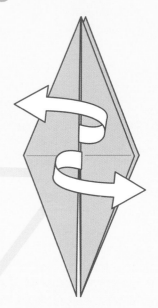

11 Extend the valley crease (formed in step 5) across the paper. Pleat downward on the diagonal.

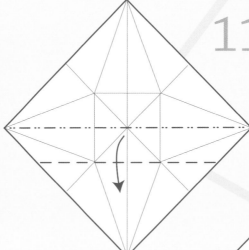

12 Follow the creases carefully to collapse the paper on the right.

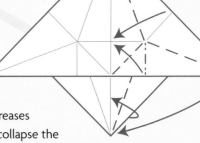

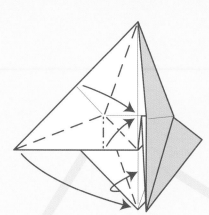

13 Repeat the last step on the left side.

14 Fold the top flap to the left so it matches the dotted line. Crease only up to the vertical then unfold. Repeat on the other side.

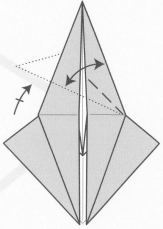

15 Lift and squash open the lower left flap, using only the creases shown. Check the next drawing. (See tip, page 77.)

16 This is the result. Repeat on the right side.

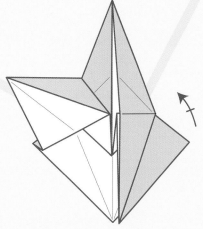

17 Lift the wings out of the way to make the two valley creases shown through the triangular flap. Turn the paper over.

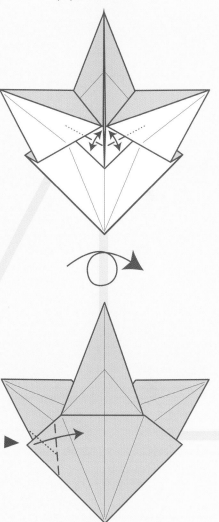

18 Make the valley fold through the upper layer and another on the dotted line, squashing the paper neatly.

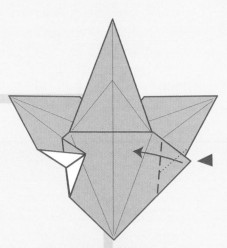

19 This is the result. Repeat on the other side.

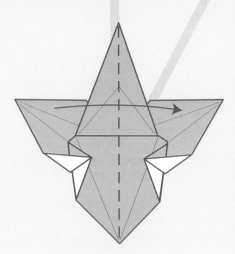

20 Fold in half from left to right.

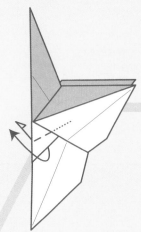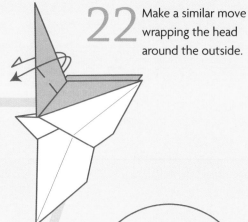

22 Make a similar move wrapping the head around the outside.

21 Open the model slightly and "flip" the flap upward on existing creases.

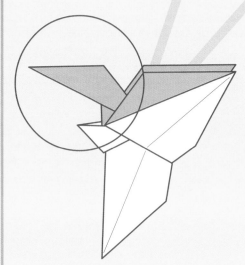

23 The model so far. Now we focus on the circled area.

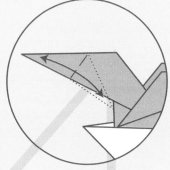

24 Fold the tip back to match the dotted line, crease and unfold. (See tip.)

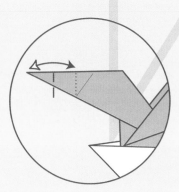

25 Fold the tip to the dotted line, crease and unfold.

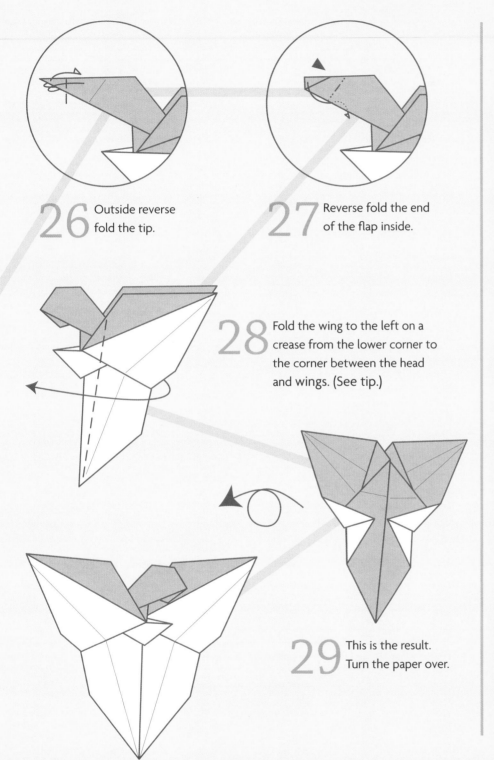

26 Outside reverse fold the tip.

27 Reverse fold the end of the flap inside.

28 Fold the wing to the left on a crease from the lower corner to the corner between the head and wings. (See tip.)

29 This is the result. Turn the paper over.

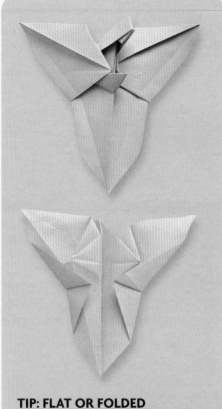

TIP: FLAT OR FOLDED

Step 12 is slightly unusual, but by no means difficult. Just begin to make all indicated creases at the same time and the layers will fall into place. Step 15 is another example of a "swivel" fold, there the paper is moved to a new location then flattened into place. Steps 24-27 can be varied to produce different faces.

Step 28 opens up one of the wings so the model can lie flat. You can, of course, miss this step out and leave the angel folded in half, which allows you to fasten it to a corner, as shown in the photo on page 72.

Angel of Peace

Frantic modern living or tensions at work or home can wear you down – in which case, turn to this angel to still your mind and bring about peace and serenity.

"Let us not be justices of the peace, but angels of peace."

ST THERESE OF LISIEUX
(1873–1897)

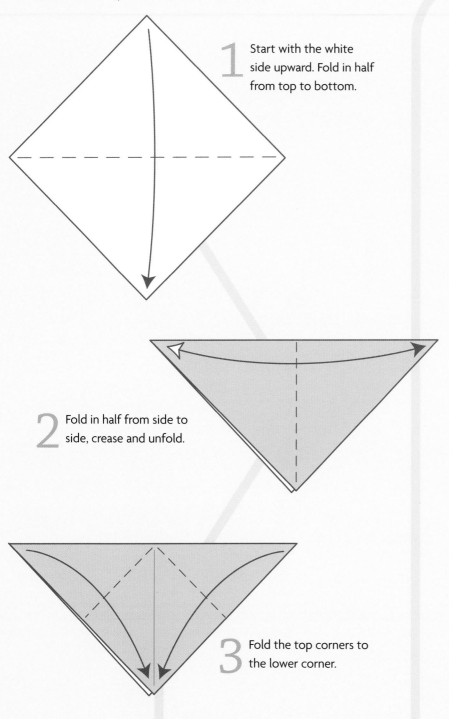

1 Start with the white side upward. Fold in half from top to bottom.

2 Fold in half from side to side, crease and unfold.

3 Fold the top corners to the lower corner.

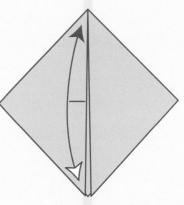

4 Fold the lower left corner to the top, make a pinch to mark half way.

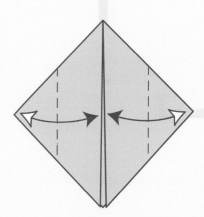

5 Fold left and right corners to the pinch, crease and unfold.

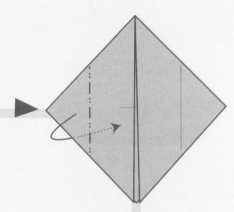

6 Inside reverse the left corner into the model.

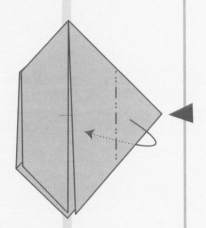

7 Repeat on the right side.

8 Fold the flap on the left across to the right.

9 Fold the lower edge of the same flap to lie on the vertical edge. (See tip, page 83.)

10 Open the right flap out.

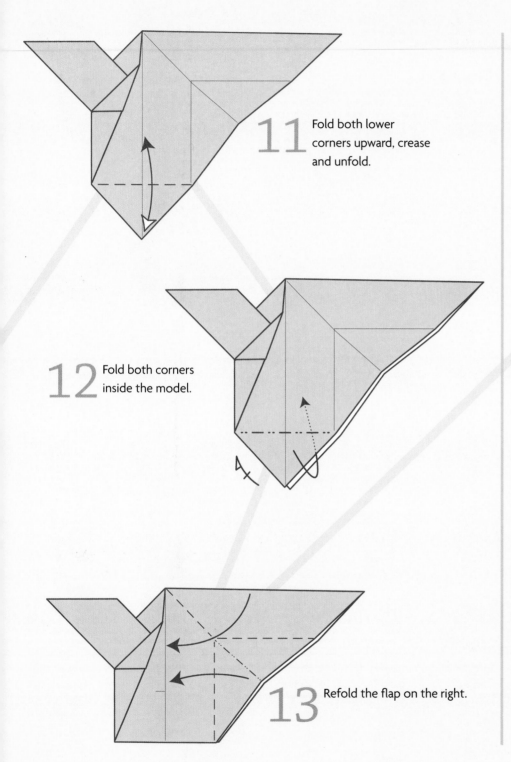

11 Fold both lower corners upward, crease and unfold.

12 Fold both corners inside the model.

13 Refold the flap on the right.

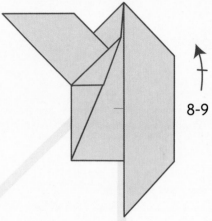

14 Repeat steps 8-9 on the right side.

8-9

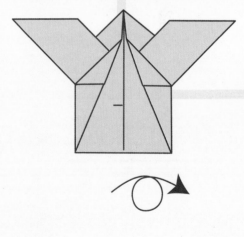

15 This is the result. Turn the paper over.

16 Fold from the lower corners, so the upper corners meet on the vertical centre.

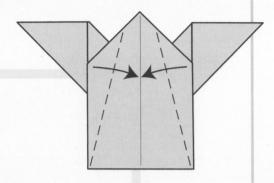

17 This is the result. We now focus on the circled area.

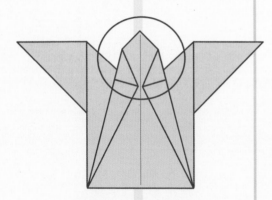

18 Fold the model in half, pinching in the creases shown.

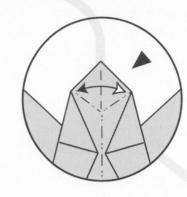

19 Make two small valley folds to wrap the top of the head forward.

20 Fold the right edge over the folded edge, gently shaping the top into a curve. Repeat on the left.

21 Reinforce the central mountain crease. Turn the model over. (See tip.)

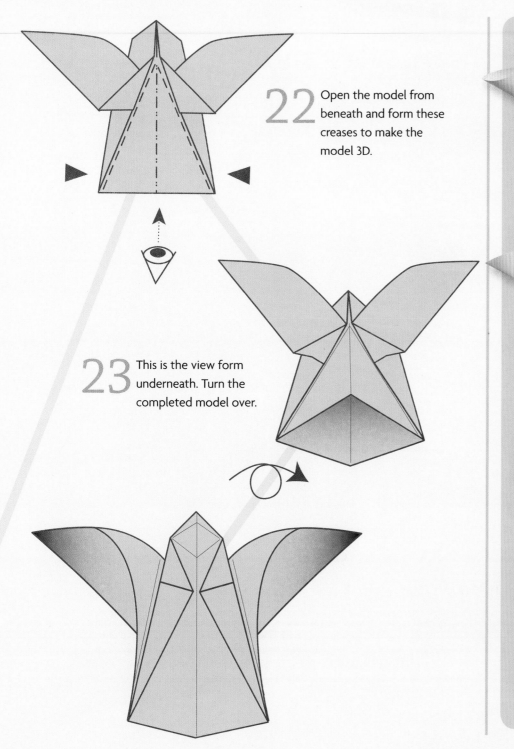

22 Open the model from beneath and form these creases to make the model 3D.

23 This is the view form underneath. Turn the completed model over.

TIP: THINKING AHEAD

You might wonder at step 9 why the instructions did not simply say "repeat on the other side". The reason is that folding the lower triangles up inside the model (in step 12) is much more difficult to do once both wings have been folded.

Step 20 requires some delicacy when folding – you don't want to have the wing shaped using a sharp crease, so try to encourage a smooth curve at this point. Step 21 requires you to open the model from underneath so that a mountain crease is formed at the front and the back of the model, at the same time.

Guardian Angel

This classic angel looks down on us with compassion – fanning his wings sometimes to cool our passions and sometimes to stoke them, as required.

"These things I warmly wish for you: someone to love, some work to do, a bit o' sun, a bit o' cheer, and a guardian angel always near."

IRISH BLESSING

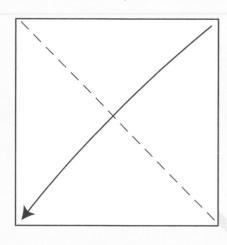

1 Start with a square, white side upward. Fold in half on a diagonal crease.

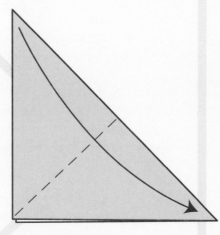

2 Fold the top left corner to the lower right corner.

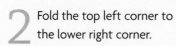

3 Fold a single corner from right to left. Repeat the fold underneath..

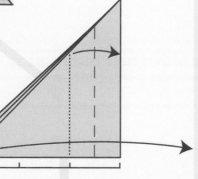

4 Fold the flap to the right so that an imaginary one-third crease lies on the right vertical edge. Repeat on the underside. (See tip, page 89.)

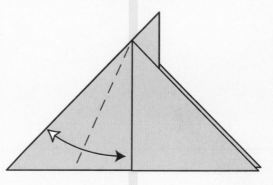

5 Fold the left edge to the nearest vertical edge, crease firmly and unfold.

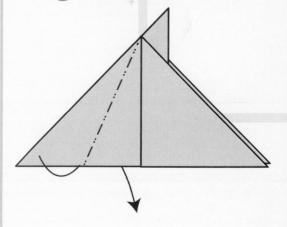

6 Inside reverse fold the same edge.

7 Fold the left flap over, crease and unfold. Repeat underneath.

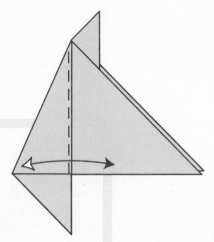

8 Unfold to the left to step 2 and rotate to the position shown in the illustration.

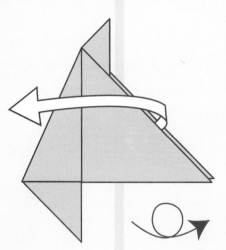

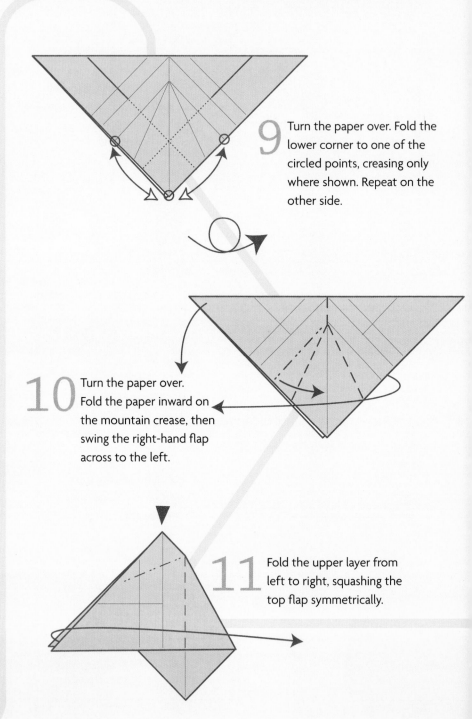

9 Turn the paper over. Fold the lower corner to one of the circled points, creasing only where shown. Repeat on the other side.

10 Turn the paper over. Fold the paper inward on the mountain crease, then swing the right-hand flap across to the left.

11 Fold the upper layer from left to right, squashing the top flap symmetrically.

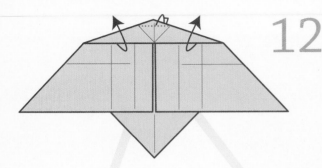

12 Lift the flap up slightly, forming a valley crease on the underside along the dotted line. (See tip, page 89.)

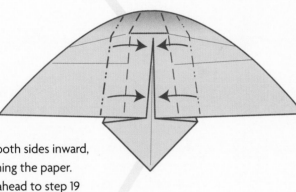

13 Pleat both sides inward, flattening the paper. Look ahead to step 19 to show the underside after the last two steps.

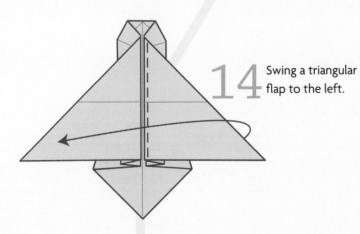

14 Swing a triangular flap to the left.

15 Make a crimp using the horizontal crease. A new valley crease forms where the dotted line lies.

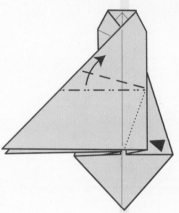

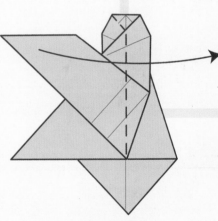

16 Swing the flap to the right.

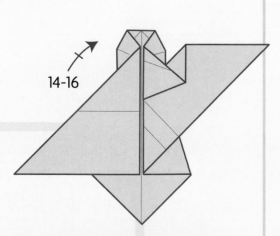

14-16

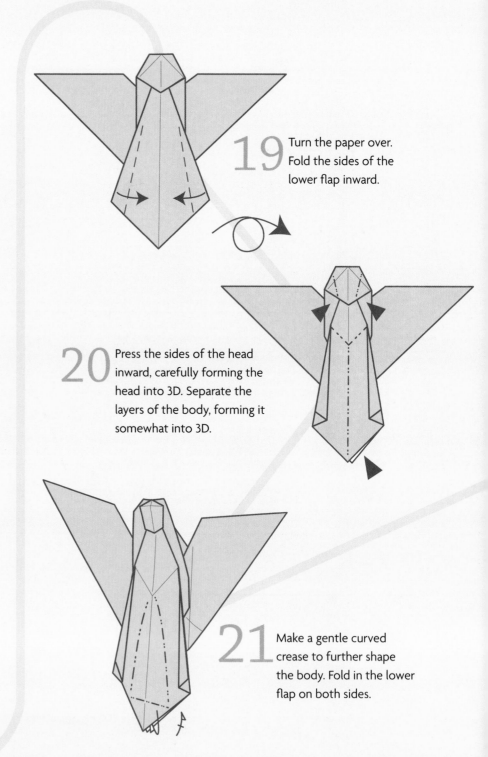

17 Repeat steps 14-16 on the left-hand wing.

19 Turn the paper over. Fold the sides of the lower flap inward.

20 Press the sides of the head inward, carefully forming the head into 3D. Separate the layers of the body, forming it somewhat into 3D.

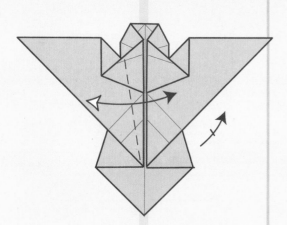

18 Make a crease through all layers of the wing. Repeat on the other side.

21 Make a gentle curved crease to further shape the body. Fold in the lower flap on both sides.

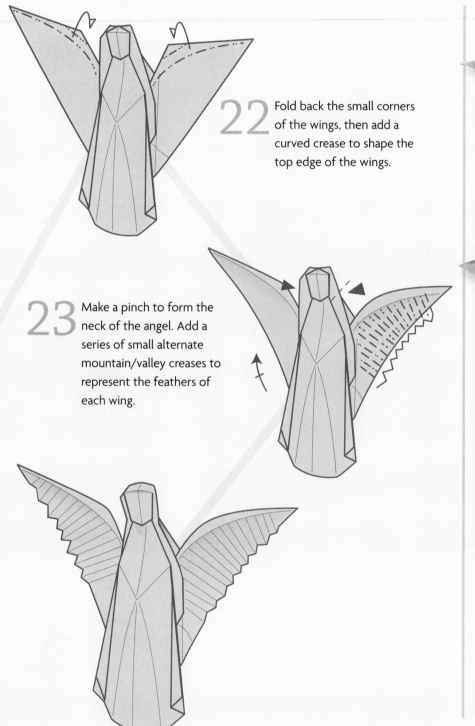

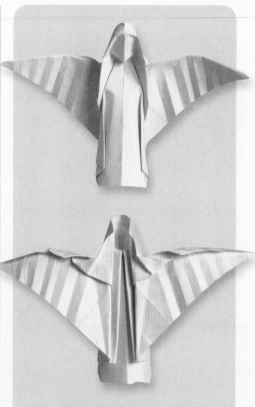

22 Fold back the small corners of the wings, then add a curved crease to shape the top edge of the wings.

23 Make a pinch to form the neck of the angel. Add a series of small alternate mountain/valley creases to represent the feathers of each wing.

TIP: PROPORTIONS

This is one of the more complex designs in the book, and there are several steps that require time and patience to master. Steps 12 and 13 require you to open the model slightly and re-form the pleats made earlier at step 4. A small corner is folded downward underneath, which is not revealed until you turn the paper over at step 19. The overall proportions of the model are decided by the fold made in step 4, so you may wish to experiment by adjusting this fold slightly. A larger square of paper will make life easier.

Angel of Prayer

Find comfort and solace through making and gazing upon this serene angel in an attitude of thoughtful prayer – definitely one for the top of your Christmas tree.

"But if these beings guard you, they do so because they have been summoned by your prayers."

ST AMBROSE
(C. 340–397 AD)

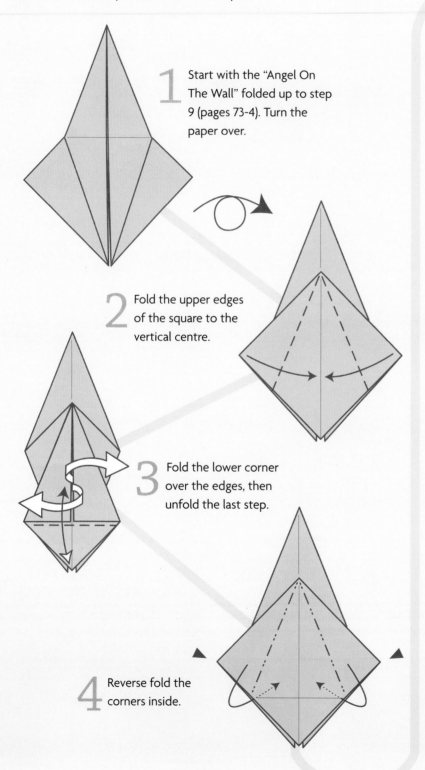

1 Start with the "Angel On The Wall" folded up to step 9 (pages 73-4). Turn the paper over.

2 Fold the upper edges of the square to the vertical centre.

3 Fold the lower corner over the edges, then unfold the last step.

4 Reverse fold the corners inside.

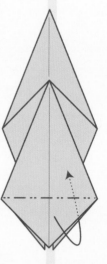

5 Fold the lower corner inside.

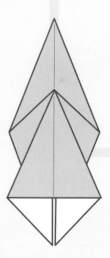

6 This is the result. Turn the paper over.

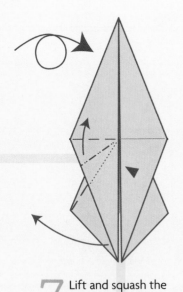

7 Lift and squash the lower left flap.

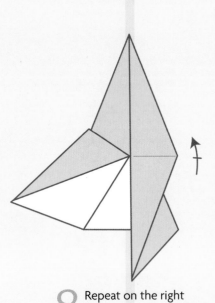

8 Repeat on the right side.

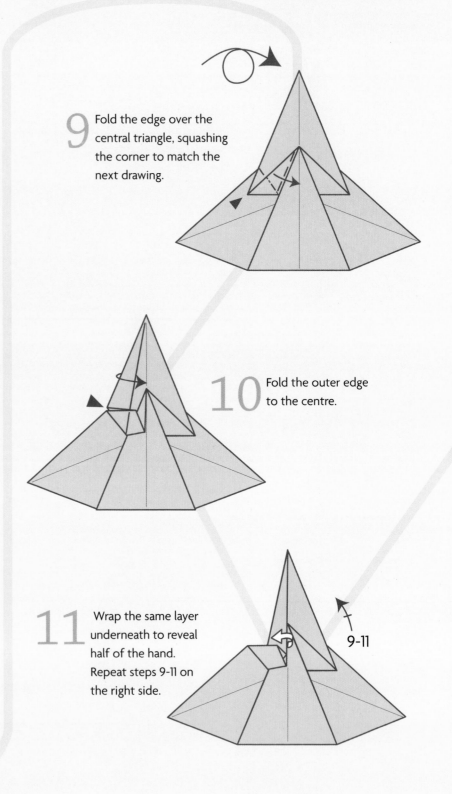

9 Fold the edge over the central triangle, squashing the corner to match the next drawing.

10 Fold the outer edge to the centre.

11 Wrap the same layer underneath to reveal half of the hand. Repeat steps 9-11 on the right side.

9-11

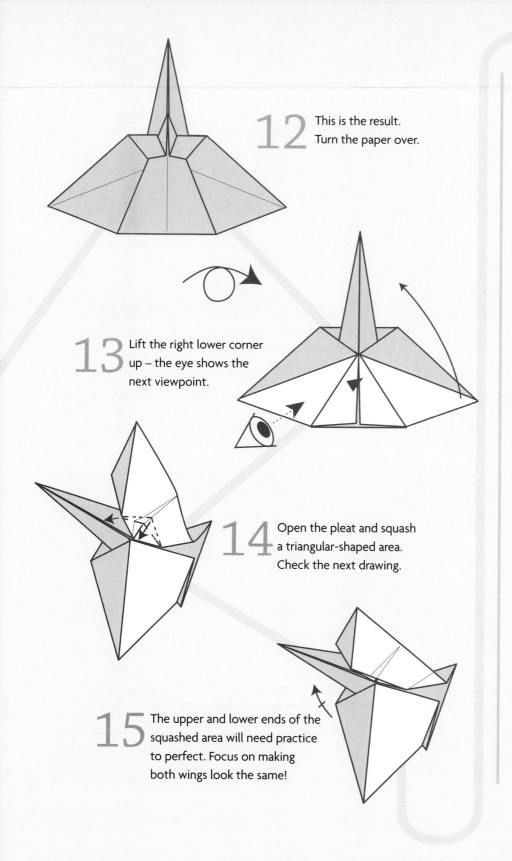

12 This is the result. Turn the paper over.

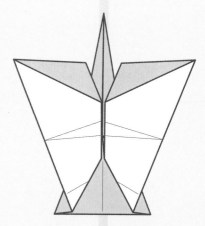

13 Lift the right lower corner up – the eye shows the next viewpoint.

14 Open the pleat and squash a triangular-shaped area. Check the next drawing.

15 The upper and lower ends of the squashed area will need practice to perfect. Focus on making both wings look the same!

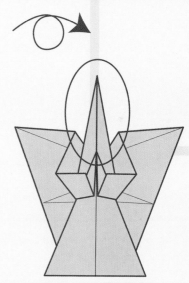

16 This is the result. Turn the paper over.

17 We now focus on the head area.

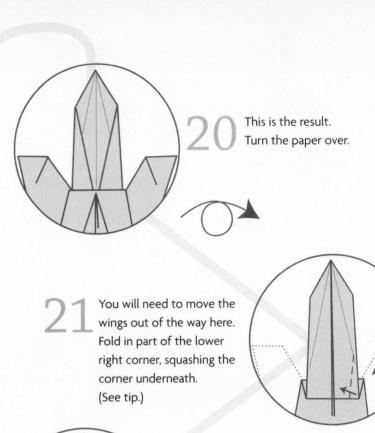

20 This is the result. Turn the paper over.

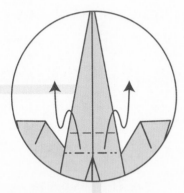

18 Pleat the head down behind.

21 You will need to move the wings out of the way here. Fold in part of the lower right corner, squashing the corner underneath. (See tip.)

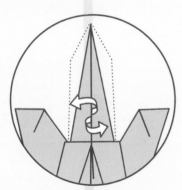

19 Ease out the layers to the dotted line. Flatten when in place.

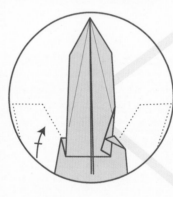

22 This is the result. Repeat on the left. Turn the paper over.

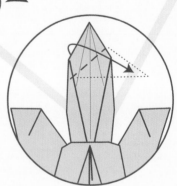

23 Fold the top of the head to the right.

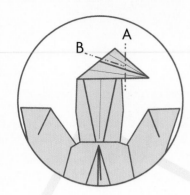
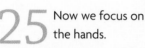

24 Make folds A and B in turn to shape the top of the head.

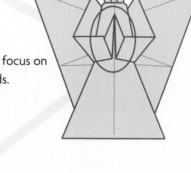

25 Now we focus on the hands.

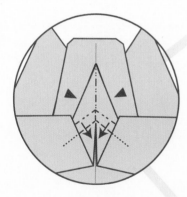

26 This step is complex and can be missed out, but it's worth the effort. Make two pleats, folding the hands down then back up again. Squeeze the sides together.

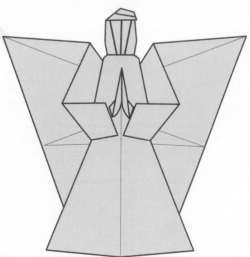

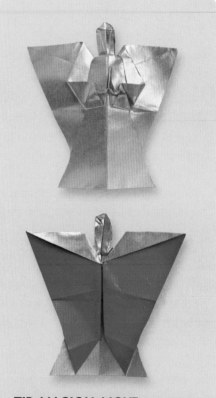

TIP: MAGICAL MOVE

Don't attempt this design until you have made all the others in the book. You will need to fold and re-fold to achieve good results. To begin with, just aim to finish the model, regardless of how it looks. Then, you can re-fold and concentrate on finesse rather than working out what to do. Starting with a larger sheet of paper will help.

Step 21 requires quite small folds: using slightly thinner paper will help. Step 26 will take some doing, but as an origami move, it's almost magical, producing two hands in prayer.

Taking it further

If you have enjoyed folding these models and wish to study origami further, there are many websites offering both diagrams and folding hints. Most countries in the world have their own origami societies, with associated websites. Here are two of the oldest and best-established societies:

UK: www.britishorigami.info
USA: www.origamiusa.org

By joining one (or more!) of these groups, you will receive regular magazines packed with model diagrams, articles, photos of the latest designs and much more. You can also attend national conventions or conferences, organized almost everywhere in the world. There is also an electronic mailing list free for anyone to subscribe to, whose details are given here:

http://lists.digitalorigami.com/mailman/listinfo/origami

Following diagrams on a screen is okay, but many people feel the best way to learn a model is from a book. Nowadays, there are many thousands of books on offer, from simple to highly complex. Here are a few that will give you a lot to fold and to consider:

Origami Design Secrets by Robert Lang
Origami Omnibus by Kunihiko Kasahara
Roses, Origami & Math by Toshikazu Kawasaki
Origamido by Michael LaFosse
Spiral by Tomoko Fuse
World's Best Origami by Nick Robinson
Teach Yourself Origami by Robert Harbin

Origami Polyhedra Design by John Montroll
Eric Joisel – the Magician of Origami by Makoto Yamaguchi
Some of these books are not cheap, but well worth investing in. As a beginner, it is worth buying an affordable book and folding your way through it for the experience.

If you'd like to learn more about angels, visit Chrissie Astell's website at www.angellight.co.uk
Nick Robinson's website is at www.origami.me.uk

Credits
The models have been included by kind permission of the creators: Neal Elias (Angel On The Wall & Angel Of Prayer), Max Hulme (Guardian Angel), David Wires (Angel Of Peace & Table Place Card Angel), Michel Grand (Angel Letter), Francis Ow (Love Heart Angel) and Evi Binzinger (Gift Box Angel). All other designs are by the author.

Acknowledgments
I would like to thank the creators listed above and also the following: all the staff at Duncan Baird for their help in bringing this project to life; Wayne Brown, who did a sterling job proof-reading the diagrams; my wife (who still doesn't realize how lucky she is); my beautiful children for keeping my feet grounded; Ruby and Matilda (our moggies); Dan and Nick from my rock band sixquid; Pete and Matt from Zugzwang; Sascha, Kristin, Joan and all at Origami Didaktiks; all my friends in the British Origami Society and the wider international origami world for their friendship and inspiration.
The book is dedicated to my good friend Martyn Bailey.